The Holdco Guide

How Entrepreneurs Structure &
Build a Holding Company That Lasts

Peter Kang

The Holdco Guide: How Entrepreneurs Structure & Build a Holding Company That Lasts © Copyright 2025 Peter Kang

All rights reserved. No part of this publication may be reproduced, distributed or transmitted in any form or by any means, including photocopying, recording, or other electronic or mechanical methods, without the prior written permission of the publisher, except in the case of brief quotations embodied in critical reviews and certain other noncommercial uses permitted by copyright law.

Although the author and publisher have made every effort to ensure that the information in this book was correct at press time, the author and publisher do not assume and hereby disclaim any liability to any party for any loss, damage, or disruption caused by errors or omissions, whether such errors or omissions result from negligence, accident, or any other cause.

Adherence to all applicable laws and regulations, including international, federal, state, and local governing professional licensing, business practices, advertising, and all other aspects of doing business in the US, Canada, or any other jurisdiction, is the sole responsibility of the reader and consumer.

Neither the author nor the publisher assumes any responsibility or liability whatsoever on behalf of the consumer or reader of this material. Any perceived slight of any individual or organization is purely unintentional.

The resources in this book are provided for informational purposes only and should not be used to replace the specialized training and professional judgment of a health care or mental health care professional.

Neither the author nor the publisher can be held responsible for the use of the information provided within this book. Please always consult a trained professional before making any decision regarding treatment of yourself or others.

For more information, email peter@peterkang.com.

ISBN: 979-8-90057-058-7 - Ebook
ISBN: 979-8-90057-059-4 - Paperback
ISBN: 979-8-90057-060-0 - Hardcover

TABLE OF CONTENTS

Introduction: From Operator to Holdco Enthusiast	5
I. What is a Holding Company?	9
II. Comparing Holdco Models	11
III. Sector-Specific Holding Companies	15
IV. Key Performance Metrics for a Holdco	33
V. Anatomy of a Holdco: Cash Flow, Reinvestment, and Growth	47
VI. The Investor Lens: Why Multi-Decade Compounders Win	53
VII. Capital Structure and Governance Foundations	57
VIII. Compensation and Incentive Structures in Opco and Holdco Leadership	70
IX. When Holdcos Fail: Patterns, Signals, and Lessons	80
X. Build a Holdco Workshop	85
XI. Private Equity's Holdco Evolution	91
XII. Superacquirers	95
XIII. Creator Holdcos and Personal Holdcos	99
Endnotes	105
More Holdco Resources	121
Appendix: More Examples of Sector-Specific Holdcos	125
Acknowledgements	137
About the Author	139

INTRODUCTION

From Operator to Holdco Enthusiast

For more than fifteen years, my professional identity was an agency operator. I hired creatives and engineers, chased new clients, worried about payroll, and measured success in client fees. The only "holding companies" (holdcos) I noticed were the big advertising networks buying digital shops like mine. I had little understanding of why they bought companies and what their endgame was with these acquisitions.

That changed when I began reading Berkshire Hathaway's shareholder letters and became more interested in the ways businesses worked. I devoured founder biographies and read books that exposed me to all kinds of businesses. *The Outsiders* by William Thorndike Jr. and *Lessons from the Titans* by Scott Davis, Carter Copeland, and Rob Wertheimer helped me better understand the power of capital allocation and transformative mergers and acquisitions (M&A) in building businesses. These books also happened to feature some of the most impressive holding companies out there.

I began tracking Chenmark, Tiny, Enduring Ventures, and dozens of private-equity roll-ups across home services, marketing, and healthcare. I learned about their M&A activities, the use of leverage, and the expansion of multiples tied to the scale of earnings before interest, taxes, depreciation, and amortization (EBITDA).

I quickly learned that these were also holding companies—entities that own multiple operating companies. What I found interesting about the holdco structure was that it made capital allocation decisions seem very explicit: Every dollar of free cash flow must be consciously reinvested, distributed, or held to create higher future returns.

Seeing that clarity in action helped me connect the dots between the agency profits we produced and the long-run value of the businesses we owned.

At the same time, my co-founder Sei-Wook Kim and I took our first steps toward Barrel Holdings. We spun out two agency businesses from our original agency, Barrel. Vaulted Oak and BX Studio had their own profit and loss (P&L) statements and began with modest investments. In a short period, they became cash-flow-generating businesses that allowed us to take bets on more agency business concepts, eventually leading to our first acquisition. Sei-Wook and I saw great potential in this model and formally transitioned out of the day-to-day of agency operations in order to work on the holdco full-time.

Since then, I've tried to study the holdco model more deeply and expose myself to as many holdcos as possible. This guide is a result of my studies.

This book does not make the argument that forming a holdco is the only, or even the best, path for every entrepreneur. Instead, it makes a simpler claim: Studying holding companies is one of the fastest ways to learn disciplined capital allocation and intentional business architecture. A decentralized software collector like Constellation, an operational system such as Danaher, or a diversified owner like Brookfield each turns abstract finance theory into concrete, observable practice. Whether you eventually build a parent entity or keep a single P&L, the underlying principles remain the same. My hope is that the following pages will help you:

- **Understand what fuels compounding:** retained cash, high returns on new capital, and a shock-proof balance sheet.
- **Apply those principles:** whether that means funding a new product, wiping out debt sooner, or buying a company that unlocks growth.
- **Think like an operator *and* an investor:** because lasting success takes sharp execution and smart capital moves.

Holding companies have quietly shaped the modern business landscape, from Warren Buffett's Berkshire Hathaway to Constellation Software to the new wave of indie acquirers and builders. Whether you're an investor seeking compounding returns or an entrepreneur designing an operating platform, the holding company model provides:

- Long-term ownership flexibility.
- Capital allocation power.
- Diversification with focus.
- Optionality across cycles.

This book is designed for both beginners exploring the holdco concept for the first time and seasoned operators looking to sharpen their models.

If you run a business, treat these pages as a concise primer on how a holdco perspective sharpens choices about growth, risk, and cash. If you invest, use the examples to refine your eye for true long-term compounders. And if you're simply curious, you'll see that the holdco world offers many paths, each proving there's more than one way to build lasting value.

Welcome to *The Holdco Guide*.

– Peter Kang

Rhinebeck, New York

November 1, 2025

I

What is a Holding Company?

Most business owners think in terms of one company, one P&L. A holding company challenges that instinct. It introduces a new way of thinking, one where the real power lies in ownership, capital allocation, and system design.

A holding company is a business entity (typically a corporation or LLC) formed not to sell products or services directly, but to own and oversee other businesses. Its core function is to control capital and allocate it across a portfolio of operating companies. While it may provide strategic guidance, shared services, or operating systems, the holding company itself rarely runs a P&L tied to its own products. Instead, it creates value through ownership, governance, and capital deployment.

These entities can take many forms:

- Berkshire Hathaway, perhaps the most studied holding company in history, owns dozens of businesses outright and holds equity stakes in many more. Its model is built on patient capital, decentralization, and long-term compounding.[1]

- Danaher operates very differently. It acquires operating businesses, installs its proprietary Danaher Business System, and actively manages performance through structured playbooks and key performance indicators (KPIs).[2]
- Some holding structures, especially those backed by private equity firms like Trive Capital, focus on building and scaling platform companies in fragmented industries with a plan for eventual exit.[3] This contrasts with permanent holdcos, like Berkshire Hathaway, that rarely sell their businesses.

What unites these diverse models is the shared belief that ownership, when paired with capital and judgment, can shape outcomes more profoundly than simply operating one business well.

Holding companies often share common tools and tendencies:

- They **consolidate financials** at the parent level, allowing for cleaner capital allocation decisions.
- They **use leverage strategically**, often depending on the durability of the underlying cash flows.
- They vary in **centralization**, with some tightly controlling subsidiaries and others granting near-total autonomy.
- They **optimize for different goals**, with some aiming for long-term return on invested capital (ROIC), others for free cash flow, and others for strategic control in legacy industries.

As seen here, while their structures may be similar, not all holding companies behave the same.

Next, we'll look at the different flavors of holdcos and what separates a capital allocator from an operator from a roll-up.

II

Comparing Holdco Models

The term *holding company* is often used loosely. It refers to a legal structure, not a specific strategy. In this guide, we focus on the behavioral models that actually define how holdcos create value.

After studying dozens of examples across industries, we've distilled the landscape into two core types of holdcos: **capital allocator holdcos** and **operational holdcos**.

These models are not theoretical; they show up in real businesses making real decisions about how to grow, manage, and invest. While holdcos come in all shapes and sizes, most fall squarely into one of these two strategic archetypes.

Capital Allocator Holdcos

These are the purists. Capital allocator holdcos don't acquire companies to "fix" them; they acquire companies because the economics are attractive and the people running them are excellent. The businesses are largely left alone, so long as they keep delivering. Berkshire Hathaway and Constellation Software are textbook examples. In both cases, capital allocation is the core competency.

M&A is frequent, but only under strict discipline. Managers are autonomous and headquarters are lean. Return on incremental invested capital is the guiding metric, not growth for growth's sake.

Operational Holdcos

These groups create value not just by owning businesses, but by improving them. Operational holdcos bring systems, tooling, and accountability frameworks that elevate average performers into standouts. Danaher, for example, developed an internal system so powerful—focused on lean principles and continuous improvement—that it became the company's most valuable intangible asset. Offshoots like Fortive and Roper Technologies have followed similar playbooks. These holdcos operate like a network of performance engines, with capital allocation and operational rigor working hand in hand.

Variations in Structure, Philosophy, and Time Horizon

While most holdcos behave like allocators or operators, not all are built the same. Ownership intent, capital structure, and organizational philosophy can meaningfully affect how a holdco shows up in the real world. Below are three important variations.

PE Roll-Ups: Holdcos with a Fixed Time Horizon

While technically holding companies, these are often better understood as temporary aggregators. Their goal is to acquire in bulk, integrate quickly, and exit with a multiple premium. The structure may resemble a holdco, but the mindset is time-bound (typically three to seven years). A firm like Trive Capital, for instance, might roll up regional players in manufacturing or consumer services with the intention of selling to a strategic buyer, or going into an initial public offering (IPO) for the entire platform. The businesses are expected to fit together tightly, culturally, and financially, and the central team often plays a heavy role in operations.

The "New Breed" of Holdcos

Some firms defy easy categorization—not because they don't fit the behavioral models above, but because of how they operate within them. These are often founder-led, permanently capitalized, and deeply driven by values. What unites them is a long-term ownership mindset, low integration, and a preference for autonomy over control. These are not a new "type" of holdco. Rather, they represent a modern, pragmatic expression of the core models, adapted for smaller-scale businesses, founder philosophy, or niche sectors.

Below are some frequently cited examples.

- Permanent Equity aligns closest to a capital allocator, acquiring and holding cash-generative businesses without intent to sell, but with an evergreen investor base and relational ethos.
- Tiny mirrors allocator behavior in the digital space, buying internet businesses with minimal disruption, focusing on steady cash flow.
- Chenmark, though hands-on operationally, blends ownership and management in a way that blurs traditional distinctions. It's small, self-financed, and focused on building long-term leadership from within.
- Enduring Ventures operates across real estate, services, and tech. The firm buys and builds businesses with no intention of selling, combining capital allocation discipline with entrepreneurial involvement. It applies operational

leverage selectively while maintaining a founder-friendly, mission-aligned structure.
- StoicLane epitomizes the "new breed" holding company, blending permanent capital with technology-driven operational improvements. Their seller-friendly approach contrasts sharply with traditional private equity methods, emphasizing legacy preservation and long-term integration.

Conglomerates: The Structural Ancestors

Conglomerates like GE, 3M, or Tata Group helped popularize the multi-business structure. These organizations spread across industries, sometimes strategically, sometimes opportunistically, often under one brand umbrella. While some achieved resilience through diversification, others struggled with complexity and capital misallocation. Conglomerates are not a distinct holdco model, but rather an earlier structural form. Modern holdcos often blend the diversification of conglomerates with tighter capital discipline, clearer ownership philosophy, and leaner organizational design.

In Practice

Many holdcos blend elements of multiple models. A capital allocator may eventually develop internal operating capabilities. An operational holdco may prioritize capital deployment just as rigorously. This is especially true for firms in the "new breed," which often borrow selectively across models.

It's important to remember that these categories aren't rigid, and in that fluidity, they offer a useful lens for understanding how a holdco thinks, behaves, and ultimately creates value.

In the next section, we'll look at how these behaviors play out across different industries—from software to services to infrastructure—and what makes certain strategies more effective in specific contexts.

III

Sector-Specific Holding Companies

While some holding companies pride themselves on being sector-agnostic, many of the most effective compounders focus deeply on a single industry. Specialization creates its own compounding advantages: It sharpens acquisition criteria, accelerates post-merger integration, and helps leadership teams speak the same operational language across entities. Patterns emerge faster, mistakes shrink in impact and cost, and synergies become repeatable rather than theoretical.

By concentrating on a specific sector, a holdco can build real structural leverage:

- **Operational depth** makes it easier to spot underperforming businesses, identify high-leverage improvement areas, and benchmark KPIs across the portfolio.
- **Economies of scale** emerge in everything from procurement and staffing to software systems and compliance.
- **Strategic coherence** strengthens investor narratives and increases the odds of successful downstream exits, particularly in roll-up or hybrid models.

- **Valuation arbitrage** becomes possible when consolidating fragmented industries where sellers are trading at 4–6x EBITDA and the platform eventually commands a premium multiple.

Of course, concentration has its downsides. A sector-specific holdco inherits the cyclicality and regulatory risks of its chosen field. External factors such as a downturn in consumer sentiment, a new healthcare reimbursement rule, or a spike in interest rates can ripple across an entire portfolio. Diversification by geography, customer mix, or business model can help, but ultimately, niche holdcos live and die by their ability to stay one step ahead of their sector's maturity curve.

What follows are examples of sector-specific holding companies across select industries, from marketing and consumer to software and restaurants. They show the varied ways long-term owners build power within, and sometimes beyond, a single vertical.

Note: Classifications reflect operating and capital structure as of publication. In some cases, private equity involvement or public ownership may exist alongside a long-term or independent operating philosophy. For additional industry sectors and holdco examples, please see the appendix.

Marketing and Advertising Services Holdcos

The marketing and advertising sector has long been fertile ground for holding companies, driven by fragmented agency ecosystems, the need for specialized services, and opportunities for operational synergies. Successful holdcos in this space master the balance between centralized efficiencies and agency-level autonomy, ensuring creative independence isn't sacrificed for scale.

However, recent trends toward digital transformation, agile service models, and client demands for transparency have pressured traditional agency holding company models, prompting new players to reimagine the balance between scale and specialization.

WPP: Scale, Complexity, and the Struggles of the Traditional Model

WPP, historically one of the most prominent global agency holding companies, built its empire by acquiring numerous specialized agencies such as Ogilvy, VMLY&R, AKQA, GroupM, and Hill+Knowlton.[1] The traditional WPP approach involves centralized financial operations, shared real estate, global media buying, and procurement leverage, while largely maintaining agency-level operational autonomy.

While this approach has historically enabled WPP to capture large global accounts and achieve significant economies of scale, the model has recently come under pressure. The complexity and bureaucratic structure of managing hundreds of individual agencies have often resulted in slower response times, reduced flexibility, and higher costs. Additionally, WPP's traditional reliance on large, media-driven accounts has exposed vulnerabilities as advertising dollars shift increasingly toward digital, agile, and direct-to-consumer strategies.

WPP's struggles have also included client demands for greater transparency and efficiency, increased competition from agile digital-native firms, and the ongoing difficulty of coordinating cohesive solutions across independent-minded agencies. These challenges underscore the need for traditional agency holdcos to rapidly adapt their operating models to align with changing market expectations.

Stagwell Group: Digital-First Integration as a Response to Market Shifts

In sharp contrast to WPP, Stagwell Group emerged as a digitally native alternative, explicitly designed to address the shortcomings of legacy networks. Stagwell prioritizes targeted integration around digital capabilities, shared technology infrastructure, data analytics, and performance media, while still allowing agencies such as Code and Theory, Assembly, and Instrument substantial creative freedom.

Stagwell's digital-first platform facilitates agility, speed, and client transparency, qualities often cited as lacking in legacy holding companies. Its operational approach leverages integrated data analytics and martech systems, enabling agencies to collaborate effectively and respond rapidly to evolving client needs. This structure positions Stagwell to better handle industry trends toward digital marketing, direct-to-consumer strategies, and real-time optimization.[2]

Key Insights and Lessons:

- **Traditional Models Face Digital Disruption:** Legacy structures like WPP's, though powerful historically, can suffer from operational complexity and slow adaptability amid digital transformation.
- **Digital Integration Boosts Agility:** Newer models like Stagwell's demonstrate how targeted, technology-enabled integration supports faster decision-making, stronger client outcomes, and greater transparency.
- **Balancing Scale and Creativity Remains Crucial:** Both traditional and newer approaches must balance the efficiencies of scale with the imperative of nurturing creative talent and maintaining agency independence.

By contrasting WPP's recent challenges with Stagwell's digitally-integrated model, agency holding companies can better understand the shifts required to thrive in today's rapidly evolving marketing and advertising landscape.

Consumer Brands Holdcos

Consumer brands holding companies leverage trusted brands, operational discipline, and powerful distribution networks to compound value. They often manage diversified portfolios across product categories such as luxury goods, household essentials, beauty products, and beverages, using brand strength and operational efficiencies to generate sustainable growth.

Unlike some sector-agnostic holdcos, successful consumer brands holdcos typically maintain focused expertise within consumer verticals. They deploy capital thoughtfully, either to acquire undervalued brands and enhance their market position or to incubate and scale new brands internally. The central challenge lies in balancing brand autonomy with shared efficiencies, ensuring individual brands retain their unique market identities while benefiting from centralized functions like supply chain management, manufacturing, marketing, and ecommerce infrastructure.

LVMH: A Model of Capital Allocation in Luxury

LVMH Moët Hennessy Louis Vuitton exemplifies a capital allocator holdco within consumer brands. Under the strategic direction of the Arnault family, LVMH has accumulated over seventy-five semi-autonomous "maisons" across categories like fashion, jewelry, wines and spirits, and hospitality. Each brand, whether it's Louis Vuitton, Dior, Tiffany, or Dom Pérignon, retains its identity, heritage, and creative autonomy. To the average consumer, it's often unclear that these brands are owned by the same holdco, a testament to the strength of each brand.

The value creation at LVMH comes from disciplined capital recycling: mature and highly profitable maisons like Louis Vuitton provide cash flow to reinvest in emerging brands or strategic acquisitions. For instance, the acquisition of Tiffany in 2021 expanded LVMH's footprint in the high-end jewelry space, revitalizing an iconic American brand through strategic investments in marketing, retail locations, and digital capabilities. Simultaneously, back-end synergies such as real estate management, digital infrastructure, and manufacturing efficiencies quietly improve operating leverage across the group.[3]

Church & Dwight: Quiet Compounding Through Operational Efficiency

In contrast to LVMH's luxury focus, Church & Dwight illustrates the capital allocation approach within the consumer staples category. Church & Dwight quietly acquires smaller, high-margin consumer brands at attractive multiples, integrating them into a lean operating structure to capture efficiencies and drive incremental margin improvement.

Brands like Arm & Hammer, OxiClean, and Waterpik are excellent examples. Acquired at modest valuations, these brands benefit from Church & Dwight's robust supply chain capabilities, centralized procurement, and streamlined marketing spend. While each brand maintains distinct consumer positioning, operational integration boosts profitability without diluting brand equity.[4]

This consistent, disciplined approach allows Church & Dwight to reliably generate cash flow, fund additional acquisitions, and steadily compound shareholder value over decades.

Key Insights and Lessons:

- **Brand Autonomy Matters:** Successful consumer holdcos respect individual brand heritage and identity, intervening strategically rather than operationally. Autonomy fosters innovation and customer loyalty, which are essential for long-term success.

- **Operational Discipline Enhances Returns:** Consumer brands gain substantial operating leverage from centralized procurement, supply chain optimization, and shared ecommerce platforms, significantly boosting profitability without harming brand integrity.

- **Patient Capital Builds Durability:** Holdcos like LVMH and Church & Dwight illustrate how long-term, patient capital allocation, rather than aggressive cost-cutting or short-term financial engineering, leads to sustainable growth.

By mastering these principles, consumer brands holdcos quietly and steadily compound value, demonstrating the power of strategic capital allocation coupled with disciplined operational execution.

Home Services Holdcos

The home services sector, which includes property management, HVAC, plumbing, electrical, and pest control, has increasingly attracted holding company models because of its fragmented market landscape, predictable revenue streams, and resilience during economic downturns. In recent years, private equity has dramatically reshaped the industry, fueling rapid consolidation, professionalization, and the pursuit of operational efficiencies.

Successful holdcos in this sector strategically balance local autonomy—critical for customer retention and quality service—

with centralized operational improvements, such as shared procurement, technology-driven field operations, and systematic best-practice implementation.

Two illustrative examples of this evolving dynamic are FirstService, representing a permanent capital allocation approach, and TurnPoint Services, demonstrating the powerful influence of private equity in accelerating consolidation and integration.

FirstService: Disciplined Capital Allocation and Local Autonomy

FirstService exemplifies a capital allocator holdco, strategically acquiring niche property services brands and residential property management companies. Rather than pursuing rapid integration, FirstService maintains a decentralized model, allowing acquired firms to retain strong local brands, community relationships, and tailored service models.

For instance, FirstService Residential, the property management division, oversees thousands of residential communities throughout North America through locally-operated subsidiaries. Simultaneously, FirstService Brands (owner of businesses such as California Closets, CertaPro Painters, and Paul Davis Restoration) operates under a lean governance structure. FirstService allocates capital strategically to drive organic growth, pursue select acquisitions, and fund operational improvements without undermining brand distinctiveness or local decision-making.[5]

This balanced approach produces consistent cash flow and steady value compounding, leveraging the resilience and customer loyalty inherent in the home services sector.

TurnPoint Services: Accelerated Integration Driven by Private Equity

TurnPoint Services highlights the profound influence of private equity in rapidly transforming home services markets. Backed by private equity, TurnPoint has emerged as a national platform specializing in HVAC, plumbing, and electrical services. Over recent years, TurnPoint has executed over forty acquisitions, primarily acquiring locally-owned, founder-led businesses.

Unlike decentralized models, TurnPoint aggressively integrates acquisitions into a cohesive operational framework. While local brands often remain outward-facing to preserve existing customer relationships, back-office functions—including procurement, dispatch operations, technology systems, and marketing—are swiftly centralized. This approach generates immediate cost efficiencies and standardized service delivery, enhancing operational leverage across its expanding portfolio.[6,7]

Private equity's influence is evident through TurnPoint's disciplined approach to deal-making, rigorous integration timelines, and performance-focused management. The aim is clear: consolidate rapidly, professionalize operations, enhance margins, and eventually achieve significant valuation multiples at recapitalization or sale.

Key Insights and Lessons:

- **Rapid PE-Driven Consolidation:** Private equity is reshaping the home services landscape, accelerating market consolidation, standardizing operational practices, and rapidly scaling firms like TurnPoint.
- **Balancing Local Autonomy with Centralized Operations:** FirstService demonstrates a careful, decentralized capital allocation approach, preserving brand identities and local relationships. Meanwhile, TurnPoint shows how rapid

integration can swiftly unlock operational efficiencies and value creation.

- **Stable, Recession-Resilient Revenues:** Both holdcos capitalize on the inherent stability and recurring revenue of essential home services, offering strong platforms for continued compounding.

By exploring the contrasting paths of FirstService's long-term decentralized model and TurnPoint's PE-backed operational integration, the evolving landscape of home services holding companies becomes clear: Effective market consolidation can take multiple forms, each providing distinct advantages within a rapidly professionalizing sector.

Software and SaaS Holdcos

Software and Software-as-a-Service (SaaS) holdcos have emerged as powerful compounding vehicles because of their highly recurring revenues, strong customer lock-in, high gross margins, and opportunities to consolidate fragmented vertical markets. Successful holdcos in this sector typically emphasize disciplined acquisition strategies, rigorous capital allocation, and operational expertise to optimize cash flow and steadily compound value over time.

Two distinctive yet equally effective examples illustrate successful software holding company approaches: Constellation Software exemplifies a decentralized, disciplined capital allocator strategy, while Trilogy (ESW Capital) demonstrates a centralized, aggressive operational integration model focused on cost efficiencies and margin expansion.

Constellation Software: Decentralized Autonomy and Disciplined Capital Allocation

Constellation Software, founded in 1995 by Mark Leonard, is widely regarded as one of the most successful capital allocators in the software industry. Constellation specializes in acquiring niche, mission-critical software businesses, typically within highly specialized vertical markets ranging from government services and healthcare administration to transportation logistics and utilities management.

Constellation's approach prioritizes autonomy and decentralized management. It acquires businesses with strong, recurring revenue and reliable customer bases, then largely leaves existing management teams intact. Rather than imposing top-down integration, Constellation relies on its acquired companies' deep market expertise and established customer relationships. Meanwhile, the parent company provides disciplined oversight, strategic capital allocation, and rigorous performance tracking.

Capital allocation decisions are meticulously evaluated against strict ROI benchmarks, with Constellation reinvesting virtually all excess cash flow into additional acquisitions. This disciplined approach has enabled Constellation to maintain consistently high returns on incremental invested capital (ROIIC), steadily compounding shareholder value for decades.[8,9]

Trilogy/ESW Capital: Aggressive Operational Integration and Margin Expansion

Trilogy, operating under ESW Capital, pursues a highly centralized, playbook-driven approach to integrating acquired software companies. After closing, ESW consolidates leadership and shared services, standardizes processes across the portfolio, and orients product organizations toward cash generation from the installed base rather than new-logo growth. Teams are frequently rebuilt with globally distributed contractors sourced via Crossover (a recruiting platform ESW uses to staff remote talent worldwide), with tight productivity tracking, uniform workflows, and "software factory" training to normalize quality and output.

The model emphasizes speed and repeatability in sourcing and closing deals (100-plus acquisitions since 2006 are frequently cited), rapid LOIs, and fast post-close operational changes. Headquarters functions are consolidated in Austin, Texas, while portfolio companies adopt common operating metrics, cost structures, and support practices intended to lift margins and stabilize cash flow.[10]

Key Insights and Lessons:

- **Capital Allocation vs. Operational Integration:** Constellation Software exemplifies patient, decentralized capital allocation, maintaining acquired companies' autonomy, whereas Trilogy highlights rapid operational integration, centralization, and aggressive margin improvement.
- **Recurring Revenue and Customer Stickiness:** Both models leverage the high margins, stable cash flows, and customer lock-in intrinsic to mission-critical software and SaaS businesses.
- **Scalability Through Discipline:** Success in software holdcos often depends on disciplined approaches, whether capital discipline (Constellation) or operational rigor (Trilogy), ensuring sustained returns and compounding value.

Together, Constellation Software and Trilogy illustrate the breadth of strategic options available to software and SaaS holding companies, highlighting how focused execution—whether through disciplined autonomy or rigorous integration—can power substantial, long-term value creation in the software sector.

Industrial Holdcos

Industrial holding companies acquire and manage specialized manufacturing businesses, typically providing critical components, niche equipment, precision instruments, or engineered products. These businesses benefit from long-standing customer relationships, specialized market leadership, and consistent demand across economic cycles. Effective industrial holdcos typically focus on disciplined operational frameworks, often deploying strategic centralization or decentralized autonomy, to drive continuous improvement, margin expansion, and durable compounding.

Two prominent examples clearly illustrate these strategies: Danaher Corporation, known for its tightly integrated operating system, and Illinois Tool Works (ITW), exemplifying decentralized autonomy combined with disciplined capital allocation.

Danaher Corporation: Systematic Integration and the Danaher Business System (DBS)

Danaher Corporation exemplifies a highly integrated operational holdco, renowned for its structured and disciplined approach known as the Danaher Business System (DBS). Danaher strategically acquires specialized industrial and life sciences businesses, such as diagnostic equipment manufacturers, life-sciences instrumentation firms, and precision technology providers, and rapidly integrates them into its proprietary operating framework.

DBS provides acquired businesses with standardized processes for continuous improvement, lean manufacturing, quality management, and operational excellence. Acquired companies swiftly adopt the DBS methodology, aligning processes, systems, and metrics company-wide to systematically boost productivity, improve quality, and expand profit margins.[11]

This rigorous operational integration has allowed Danaher to generate exceptional and consistent returns on capital, strong free cash flow, and ongoing margin improvements. Its integrated model has become an industry benchmark for driving operational excellence and disciplined execution, underpinning decades of sustained growth and shareholder value creation.

Illinois Tool Works (ITW): Decentralized Autonomy and the 80/20 Rule

Illinois Tool Works (ITW) illustrates an alternative industrial holdco strategy emphasizing decentralized autonomy, disciplined capital allocation, and targeted operational excellence. ITW manages a diversified portfolio of specialized manufacturing businesses, including automotive components, industrial packaging, welding equipment, food equipment, and testing instruments.

Unlike Danaher's highly centralized DBS approach, ITW follows a decentralized operating philosophy anchored by its proprietary "80/20 Front-to-Back Process." This disciplined methodology directs each business unit to focus resources and management attention specifically on the roughly 20 percent of customers and products that generate approximately 80 percent of revenue and profitability. The process systematically reduces operational complexity by streamlining product portfolios, optimizing production, and intensifying customer focus to drive sustainable organic growth.[12]

Each ITW business operates with considerable independence, maintaining close customer relationships, responding swiftly to local market conditions, and tailoring operations around core, high-margin opportunities. Additionally, ITW's Customer-Back Innovation approach ensures that product development aligns closely with top customers' specific needs, leading to differentiated offerings and robust market positions.

At the corporate level, ITW emphasizes rigorous capital allocation discipline, strategic oversight, and consistent operational benchmarking. This decentralized yet highly disciplined structure fosters an entrepreneurial culture characterized by ownership mentality, agility, and market responsiveness. The result is superior margin performance, strong cash flow generation, and consistently attractive returns for shareholders across ITW's diversified industrial portfolio.

Key Insights and Lessons:

- **Operational Integration vs. Decentralized Autonomy:** Danaher's highly structured DBS model contrasts sharply with ITW's decentralized approach, highlighting two effective strategies for achieving continuous improvement and sustained profitability.

- **Disciplined Processes and Continuous Improvement:** Both Danaher and ITW consistently apply rigorous frameworks (DBS for Danaher, 80/20 for ITW) to achieve operational excellence, optimize resource allocation, and drive long-term value creation.

- **Specialized Expertise and Durable Customer Relationships:** Industrial holdcos succeed by preserving specialized market leadership, deep technical expertise, and strong customer relationships within their operating companies, leveraging these strengths to maintain stable cash flow and sustainable growth.

By comparing Danaher's centralized, systematic integration with ITW's decentralized, entrepreneurial autonomy, we see two powerful and complementary approaches to compounding long-term value within specialized industrial markets, each uniquely suited to leveraging operational discipline and market-specific expertise.

Restaurant Group Holdcos

Restaurant holding companies consolidate multiple dining concepts, leveraging brand portfolios, operational efficiencies, shared infrastructure, and diverse market segments to generate stable cash flows and sustainable growth. Successful restaurant holdcos typically balance operational centralization, such as unified procurement, technology platforms, and strategic marketing, with distinct brand identities and tailored customer experiences.

Two illustrative examples showcasing effective yet distinct strategies within the restaurant sector are Darden Restaurants, representing a centralized operational model emphasizing company-owned locations, and Restaurant Brands International (RBI), exemplifying a decentralized, franchise-focused, capital allocation approach.

Darden Restaurants: Centralized Operations and Company-Owned Scale

Darden Restaurants exemplifies a tightly integrated operational holdco approach, primarily owning and operating its restaurant concepts. Their properties include well-known brands such as Olive Garden, LongHorn Steakhouse, Cheddar's Scratch Kitchen, Yard House, The Capital Grille, and Seasons 52.

Darden emphasizes operational excellence through centralized capabilities in procurement, real estate management, technology infrastructure, labor analytics, and menu development. Its scale enables Darden to achieve significant efficiencies, maintain rigorous quality control, and offer consistent dining experiences across thousands of company-owned locations nationwide. Centralized systems allow Darden to optimize supply-chain costs, streamline operations, and consistently execute strategic marketing initiatives across its portfolio.[13]

By managing restaurant operations centrally, Darden can quickly adapt to market changes, maintain strong financial discipline, and continuously enhance operational margins. This approach enables predictable cash flow generation, sustainable profitability, and stable growth.

Restaurant Brands International (RBI): Franchise-Driven Capital Allocation and Decentralized Autonomy

Restaurant Brands International (RBI), owner of leading quick-service restaurant brands such as Burger King, Tim Hortons, Popeyes, and Firehouse Subs, employs a capital allocation-focused franchise model emphasizing decentralized operational autonomy.

Unlike Darden's centrally managed company-owned locations, RBI primarily operates through franchise partnerships, allowing local franchisees to manage day-to-day operations, adapt menus regionally, and tailor service to local customer preferences. RBI's role centers on strategic capital allocation, brand stewardship, franchise support, and leveraging scale through global marketing campaigns, supply-chain efficiencies, technology investments, and brand revitalization initiatives.[14]

The franchise model provides RBI with stable, recurring royalty revenues, minimal operational complexity at the corporate level, and substantial free cash flow. RBI strategically deploys this cash flow for shareholder-friendly activities such as dividends, share buybacks, and further acquisitions or reinvestments aimed at enhancing long-term growth.

Key Insights and Lessons:

- **Operational Integration vs. Franchise Autonomy:** Darden's centralized operational management contrasts sharply with RBI's decentralized franchise approach, illustrating two effective paths to growth and profitability in restaurant holding companies.

- **Scale, Efficiency, and Brand Strength:** Both models effectively leverage scale and strong brand portfolios, whether through operational control (Darden) or franchise-driven capital allocation (RBI), generating stable revenues and robust market positions.
- **Stable Cash Flows and Strategic Capital Deployment:** Restaurant holdcos succeed by generating consistent cash flows through scalable operations or royalty income, strategically deploying capital to drive sustained growth, brand strength, and long-term shareholder value.

These two restaurant group holdcos illustrate complementary pathways to durable, profitable, and sustainable growth in the highly competitive dining sector.

IV

Key Performance Metrics for a Holdco

Talk of capital allocation and reinvestment is meaningless without a way to measure impact. This chapter lays out the key financial signals that reveal whether a holding company is growing real, durable value.

A holding company lives or dies by its ability to turn today's operating cash into more cash tomorrow. Accounting profit can hide a multitude of sins, so seasoned operators watch a handful of cash-focused metrics that tell the real story of compounding.

Free Cash Flow

Free cash flow is the cash a business generates after covering its operating expenses, taxes, and required capital expenditures, including changes in working capital. It represents cash available to the company's capital providers before financing decisions. It's the actual cash available to reinvest, acquire, repay debt, or distribute to owners. FCF is the foundation of capital allocation.

Formula:

FCF = EBITDA - Capex - Changes in Working Capital - Taxes - Mandatory Debt Service

Some simplify it as Operating Cash Flow - Capex, but for holdco-level decisions, it's important to deduct working capital shifts and required debt payments to get to a figure for truly deployable capital.

FCF in Capital-Light Businesses: In businesses with minimal capex and steady working capital, like agencies or mature SaaS, EBITDA is often a good proxy for FCF. But even in these cases, watch out for timing issues—late collections or unbilled work—and tax drag, which can distort real cash availability.

What's "Good": 10%+ annual growth in FCF/share is typically considered strong. For elite compounders, 15–20%+ sustained over many years is the gold standard (e.g., Constellation Software, Berkshire, Danaher).

Example A: SaaS Business

- Revenue: $5M
- EBITDA: $1.5M
- Capex: $100k
- Working capital change: -$200k
  - AR increased by $150k (slower client payments)
  - Prepaid expenses grew by $75k (annual software contracts)
  - Offset by $25k increase in accrued expenses (delayed vendor payments)
- Taxes: $300k
  - → **FCF = $1.5M - $100k - $200k - $300k**
  - FCF Margin = $900k ÷ $5M Revenue = 18%

- Even with strong EBITDA, working capital absorbed $200k in cash—highlighting how growth can consume cash even in profitable companies.

Example B: Capital-Light Agency

- Revenue: $3M
- EBITDA: $900k
- Capex: $25k
- Working capital change: -$50k
    - AR increased by $60k (client payment delays)
    - Unbilled hours (WIP) increased by $40k
    - Offset by $50k increase in accounts payable (delayed vendor payments)
- Taxes: $225k
    → **FCF = $900k - $25k - $50k - $225k**
    FCF Margin = $600k ÷ $3M Revenue = 20%
- Here, EBITDA is a close approximation of FCF, but even a small buildup in receivables and WIP reduced the cash available to the owners. This is a reminder that even capital-light businesses can tie up cash if operations aren't tight.

FCF is what funds your future. It powers reinvestment, acquisitions, debt reduction, and distributions. If you're not consistently generating and growing FCF, you're not building a compounding business.

To improve FCF:

- Tighten billing and collections.
- Minimize work in progress (WIP) or unbilled hours.
- Keep discretionary capex low.
- Don't let operational sloppiness silently soak up cash.

Note on Free Cash Flow per Share (FCF/share): If your holdco has a shareholder structure (internal or external), tracking FCF/share shows how much cash value is accruing to each ownership unit over time.

Formula

FCF ÷ Shares Outstanding

Why it matters

If FCF is growing faster than your share count, each share is becoming more valuable. This is the clearest signal of per-share compounding. Companies like Constellation Software and Berkshire Hathaway obsess over this metric because it reveals whether capital allocation is actually increasing owner value, not just headline profits.

Return on Invested Capital (ROIC)

ROIC measures how efficiently a business turns capital into profit. It asks: For every dollar tied up in the business—whether in equipment, working capital, or intangibles—how much after-tax profit is generated annually?

Formula

ROIC = NOPAT (Net Operating Profit After Tax) ÷ Invested Capital

Invested Capital = Net Working Capital + Net Fixed Assets + Intangibles

What counts as "Invested Capital"

In capital-light businesses like agencies or SaaS firms, invested capital isn't in machines or buildings; it's mostly in working capital. This includes accounts receivable (work delivered but unpaid) and unbilled revenue (work in progress), minus payables. While not hard assets, these represent real cash tied up in operations, your "soft factory" waiting to be turned into spendable dollars.

What's "Good"

15%+ ROIC is generally the benchmark for strong capital allocators. Below 10% and you risk value stagnation or destruction.

Example A: Moderate-Capex Business (e.g., SaaS or light manufacturing)

- Revenue: $5M
- EBITDA: $1.2M
- Taxes: 25% → NOPAT = $900k
- Invested Capital:
    - Working capital: $600k
    - Capitalized software & equipment: $1.2M
    - Total Invested Capital = $1.8M
- **ROIC = $900k ÷ $1.8M = 50%**

    This is a healthy return, as each dollar tied up in the business is generating $0.50 in annual after-tax profit.

Example B: Capital-Light Agency Business

- Revenue: $3M
- EBITDA: $900k
- Taxes: 25% → NOPAT = $675k

- Invested Capital:
    - Accounts receivable: $400k
    - Unbilled revenue: $100k
    - Less accounts payable/accrued: -$250k
        → Net Working Capital = $250k
    - No capex, no inventory, no intangible assets capitalized
        → Total Invested Capital = $250k
- **ROIC = $675k ÷ $250k = 270%**

    This is not uncommon for agencies. With little capital tied up, a well-run business can generate massive returns, but the flip side is that there are fewer ways to reinvest large amounts of capital back into the business at the same return rate.

Return on Incremental Invested Capital (ROIIC)

If ROIC looks backward, ROIIC looks forward. It measures how well new capital is being deployed. This tells you whether reinvestment is actually improving the overall return profile.

Formula

ROIIC = Change in NOPAT ÷ Change in Invested Capital

What Counts as "Incremental Capital"

Incremental capital includes additional working capital (e.g., higher receivables, new hires driving WIP), capex or capitalized software, acquisitions or expansion costs, and growth investments (like standing up a new service line or vertical). It's any money not already in the baseline, now tied up to grow future profits.

What's "Good"

Sustained ROIIC of 20%+ is a clear sign the company is deploying capital effectively. If ROIIC is higher than historical ROIC, value is compounding faster.

Example A: SaaS Business Expanding into a New Vertical

- Year 1 (see previous ROIC section):
    - NOPAT = $900k
    - Invested Capital = $1.8M
    - ROIC = 50%
- Year 2:
    - The SaaS business invests $600k to enter a new vertical:
        - NOPAT = $1.2M
        - Invested Capital = $2.4M
    - → Change in NOPAT = $300k
    - → Change in Invested Capital = $600k
- **ROIIC = $300k ÷ $600k = 50%**
- Since ROIIC equals ROIC, the business is maintaining its capital efficiency while growing. If ROIIC had been 70%, it would indicate a stronger growth trajectory.

Example B: Agency Adds a Strategy Team

- Year 1 (see previous ROIC section):
    - NOPAT = $675k
    - Invested Capital = $250k
    - ROIC = 270%
- Year 2:
    - The agency invests $200k to launch a new paid media offering:

- $100k in new hires
- $50k in marketing
- $50k in operational setup and sales support
- This investment increases working capital (AR and WIP) due to new client onboarding.
- NOPAT rises to $825k
- Total Invested Capital = $450k
→ Change in NOPAT = $150k
→ Change in Invested Capital = $200k
- **ROIIC = $150k ÷ $200k = 75%**
- The agency deployed $200k into a new, trackable initiative that generated an incremental $150K in after-tax profit. Even though the original ROIC drops (now $825k ÷ $450k = 183%), the ROIIC of 75% signals a high-quality reinvestment.

Multiple on Invested Capital (MOIC)

MOIC measures the total value created from an investment relative to the original dollars put in. It's a simple but powerful way to understand whether an acquisition or growth bet has paid off, especially when you're not doing mark-to-market valuations each quarter.

Formula

MOIC = (Total Cash Returned + Current Equity Value) ÷ Capital Invested

Unlike the Internal Rate of Return (IRR), which accounts for the timing of cash flows, MOIC is time-agnostic. It tells you how much value was created, not how quickly it was created.

What's "Good"

A MOIC of 2.0x or greater within five years generally signals a successful deal. Hitting 3.0x over six to seven years is a sign of strong capital deployment, especially in lower-risk, control-based acquisitions. If your average MOIC across multiple deals climbs while your hold periods stay steady or even lengthen, it's a sign your capital is compounding efficiently without relying on exits or financial engineering.

Example: Holdco Acquires a Business

- A holdco acquires a small business for $1M total invested capital. Over four years, the business generates $1.1M in cumulative distributions back to the holdco (from profits).
- The holdco still owns the business, and it's now conservatively valued at $1.9M based on 5x EBITDA.
- **MOIC = ($1.1M cash returned + $1.9M equity value) ÷ $1M invested = 3.0x**

    This means every $1 invested has turned into $3 of value (realized + unrealized). That's a solid outcome, even without an exit. No liquidity event is required for the return to be *real* in holdco terms.

MOIC is a helpful measure for long-term, control-oriented owners like holdcos. You don't need to sell or revalue the business every year. As long as you're collecting real cash over time (distributions) and the business holds durable value (growing EBITDA, sticky clients, low churn), you can track your return on the original capital clearly and consistently.

While IRR is better for LP-backed funds with fixed lifecycles, MOIC is more intuitive for operators running permanent capital models.

High-MOIC outcomes usually come from overpaying less, holding longer, and operating better. They don't require heroic growth, just consistent cash flow and good discipline.

Look-Through Earnings and Cash Conversion

"Look-through earnings" refers to the true, cash-based profitability of the underlying operating companies, not just what shows up on the holdco's P&L. Cash conversion then measures how much of that earnings power actually becomes deployable free cash. Is the EBITDA across your portfolio turning into real cash, or is it getting stuck in the pipes?

Formula

Cash Conversion Ratio = Free Cash Flow ÷ EBITDA (at the operating company or consolidated level)

What's "Good"

A cash conversion ratio of 80–90%+ signals healthy, reliable cash generation. If FCF consistently falls below 70% of EBITDA, it's a sign that working capital, deferred reinvestment, or low-quality earnings may be eroding real value. For capital-light businesses, high conversion should be the norm.

Example: Decentralized Holdco with Three Opcos

- A holdco owns three companies:
    - Opco A: $1.2M EBITDA → $1.0M FCF
    - Opco B: $800k EBITDA → $650k FCF
    - Opco C: $500k EBITDA → $350k FCF
- Total Portfolio EBITDA = $2.5M

- Total Free Cash Flow = $2.0M
  - → Cash Conversion Ratio = $2.0M / $2.5M = 80%
- This means 80% of reported EBITDA is showing up as usable, distributable cash at the holdco level, a healthy range. The 20% shortfall may reflect timing issues, reinvestment at the opco level, or conservative cash holds for tax/working capital.

High EBITDA doesn't always mean high cash. Especially in a decentralized holdco, earnings reported by operating companies can be masked by poor collections, aggressive accruals, deferred capex, or excess payroll timing.

Cash conversion is a BS detector that reveals whether earnings are real or just optimistic accounting. Tracking this metric gives holdcos a cleaner view of which businesses are truly cash-efficient, whether reinvestment is masking liquidity risk, and how much capital is actually available for redeployment.

Note on The Float Effect: In rare cases, cash conversion can exceed 100%, particularly in businesses with float characteristics. If a business collects cash up front (e.g., prepaid retainers, subscriptions, insurance premiums) or operates on a negative working capital cycle (e.g., gets paid before it pays vendors), it can produce more cash than EBITDA—at least temporarily. This isn't financial magic; it's the result of efficient timing and business model design. For holdcos, float-generating businesses are valuable. They fund growth internally and reduce dependency on outside capital.

Balance-Sheet Resilience

Balance-sheet resilience measures how well a holdco can withstand volatility, debt burdens, and downside scenarios without putting the whole portfolio at risk. It focuses on leverage, but more importantly, the type of leverage.

Formula

Net Debt to EBITDA = (Total Debt - Cash) ÷ EBITDA

Recourse vs. Non-Recourse Debt

Not all debt carries the same risk. Recourse debt allows a lender to go after the holdco's central assets, including other operating companies, if the borrower defaults. This creates systemic risk and can jeopardize the entire portfolio. In contrast, non-recourse debt is ring-fenced: The lender can only seize assets within the specific entity that borrowed the money. If that operating company (opco) fails, the loss is contained and the rest of the holdco remains intact.

As a rule, holdcos should push debt as close to the asset as possible, avoiding parent guarantees unless absolutely necessary. This structure protects downside, preserves optionality, and ensures that no single deal can take down the whole system.

What's "Good"

A net debt to EBITDA ratio of <2.5x is considered conservative. Moderate would be about 3 to 4x, which may be appropriate for stable, cash-generating assets. Above 5x raises risk significantly, especially if earnings are volatile.

But just as important as how much debt you carry is where it sits. Separating recourse from non-recourse debt is essential.

Example: Structuring Smart Leverage

- A holdco has:
    - $1M debt tied to opco A (non-recourse)
    - $750k bank loan for a past acquisition (holdco-level, partially recourse)

- $500k cash on holdco balance sheet
- Consolidated EBITDA = $2.5M
- → Net Debt = $1.75M − $500K = $1.25M
- → Net Debt to EBITDA = $1.25M ÷ $2.5M = 0.5x
- That's a healthy leverage profile. And because a large portion of the debt is non-recourse and asset-specific, even a default wouldn't threaten the entire holdco.

Leverage can accelerate returns, but misused, it's the fastest way to blow up a holdco.

Balance-sheet resilience is about more than just interest rates or debt coverage ratios. It's about where the risk lives, how insulated each opco is, and whether the holdco can survive a hit without being forced to sell or restructure.

Bringing the Dashboard Together

Combined, these measures form a dashboard as a practical system for evaluating whether a holding company is creating durable, compounding value.

- **FCF** tells you how much cash is truly available to deploy.
- **ROIC** and **ROIIC** measure the quality of capital allocation.
- **MOIC** tracks whether past bets are delivering meaningful returns.
- **Cash conversion** ensures reported earnings are translating into actual cash.
- **Balance-sheet resilience** signals whether the system can absorb shocks without unraveling.

Example

Imagine a holdco that acquired a small business two years ago for $1.2M. Since then, it has received $900k in distributions and values the business today at $1.8M based on conservative EBITDA comps. That's a 2.25x MOIC, without needing to sell.

This cash was partially reinvested: $300k went into launching a new service line at another opco, resulting in an incremental $90k in NOPAT, a 30% ROIIC. This suggests the holdco is not just earning well on legacy assets, but also deploying new capital effectively.

Across the portfolio, the cash conversion ratio sits at 85%, signaling strong operational discipline and minimal leakage between accounting profit and actual cash. Net debt to EBITDA is 1.8x, with most of the debt non-recourse and secured at the opco level, protecting the system from cascading risk.

And most importantly, FCF per share is growing at 12% annually, with no new equity issued; each ownership unit is quietly compounding in real economic value.

This is what a healthy holdco looks like. The dashboard doesn't just track financial signals; it creates a common language for decision-making. With this in place, we can now shift focus to how value is actually built, including how cash flows through the system, how reinvestment decisions get made, and how long-term growth takes shape through deliberate capital allocation.

V

Anatomy of a Holdco: Cash Flow, Reinvestment, and Growth

Let's walk through how a holding company creates value—not in abstract theory, but in the practical mechanics of cash flow, capital allocation, and growth. This example is designed for anyone who has operated a P&L and wants to understand how the holdco structure elevates those dynamics across multiple businesses.

Meet the Holdco

Bucket Group is a simple holding company. It owns three operating businesses:

- **Canister Agency** – a digital marketing firm generating $1.2M in EBITDA
- **Pail Plumbing** – a home services business generating $800k in EBITDA
- **Crate LMS** – a SaaS product generating $500k in EBITDA

None of these businesses are new or broken. They're profitable, stable, and run with their own P&Ls. Each business has autonomy over its operations but adheres to a financial discipline set by Bucket.

- Total Portfolio EBITDA: $2.5M
- Estimated Taxes: ~$750k (30% blended effective rate)
- Opco-Level Retained Capital: ~$330k
- Free Cash Flow to Holdco: ~$1.42M

Note: Taxes are modeled assuming pass-through ownership (e.g., S corp or LLC structure) and reflect a conservative 30% blended effective rate on EBITDA. Opcos retain cash for working capital, maintenance capex, and small-scale growth initiatives.

Cash Flow Overview: Who Controls What

Each operating company retains enough cash for basic needs:

- Working capital.
- Maintenance capex.
- Pre-approved growth initiatives.

The remaining excess cash is distributed to Bucket Group, the holdco, where real capital allocation begins.

Bucket's job is to decide what to do with this $1.42M in free cash flow. Here are the four core options:

1. Reinvest Strategically

This is distinct from the reinvestment already happening at the opco level. Holdco-led reinvestment means Bucket Group deploys capital across the portfolio to fund initiatives that clear a high return threshold. Examples:

- Inject $150k into Crate LMS to expand into a new vertical.
- Fund $100k for Canister to launch a new AI-driven service.
- Incubate a new opco with $50k in seed capital.
  Total: $300k

This capital is precious (it's already been vetted and taxed) so it's used selectively, and only when ROI is compelling across the portfolio.

2. Make Acquisitions

Bucket can deploy capital into a new business entirely:

- $400k equity + $1.6M bank loan = acquisition of a $500k EBITDA pest control firm at 4x EBITDA
  Equity Deployed: $400k

This expands the portfolio's cash base and creates a new source of future cash flows.

3. Pay Down Debt

If previous acquisitions were debt-financed, part of the cash is used to deleverage:

- $200k toward principal repayment on a prior note

This lowers financial risk and increases future distributable cash.

4. Distribute to Owners or Hold Cash

Bucket can reward owners:

- $320k distributed to shareholders
- $200k held on the balance sheet for future opportunities

This preserves optionality and provides downside protection.

The Holdco Capital Allocation Model

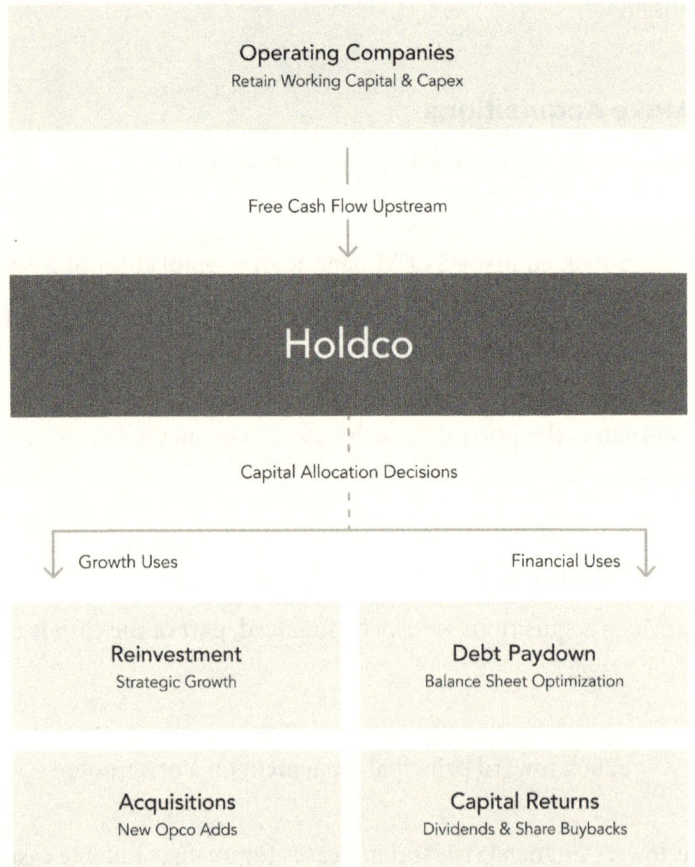

Summary: Where the Cash Went

Use of Funds	Amount
Strategic Reinvestment	$300k
Acquisition Equity	$400k
Debt Paydown	$200k
Owner Distributions	$320k
Holdco Cash Reserve	$200k
Total	$1.42M

What this illustrates is the compounding effect of disciplined capital deployment. The holdco doesn't just passively collect dividends. It reallocates capital, selectively reinvesting, acquiring cash-flowing businesses, deleveraging to reduce risk, and rewarding shareholders, while keeping enough dry powder for flexibility. Over time, these decisions drive long-term value creation far beyond what any single opco could accomplish alone.

Why Governance Matters

To ensure an opco doesn't reinvest excessively and starve the holdco of capital, Bucket uses:

- **Thresholds** – Any reinvestment above $100k requires holdco sign-off.
- **Clear KPIs** – ROI benchmarks must be defined and tracked.

- **Aligned Incentives** – Profit shares and bonuses are tied to holdco distributions.

This combination ensures local teams run lean and opportunistically, without hoarding cash or chasing vanity growth.

The Power of the Model

If Bucket compounds free cash flow by 15 to 20 percent annually through smart reinvestment and disciplined M&A, it could double its free cash in under five years, all without raising external capital.

But the model isn't magic. It works because:

- Cash flow is predictable and accessible.
- Reinvestment is intentional.
- Debt is used with discipline.
- Incentives are built for alignment.

The true power of a holding company isn't owning many businesses. It's in allocating capital across businesses. If you've ever run a company and wondered what to do with the profits (grow, buy, save, or return) then you already understand the core of what makes a holdco special. It's that same scenario, repeated across multiple P&Ls, with increasing skill.

Understanding cash flow and capital deployment is only part of the story. To truly evaluate a holdco, you need to see it through an investor's lens and understand how multi-decade compounders are built.

VI

The Investor Lens: Why Multi-Decade Compounders Win

Investors don't care about structure; they care about compounding. In 1967, Warren Buffett paid $14 million for National Indemnity, an Omaha-based insurance company.[1] Today, that single purchase contributes more than $2 billion of annual float to Berkshire Hathaway. The lesson is simple: Time, disciplined reinvestment, and aligned incentives turn ordinary cash into extraordinary wealth.

Savvy investors look for three things when they evaluate a holding company:

1. A Transparent, Repeatable Allocation Record

Investors trust groups that publish an unvarnished track record—not just glossy case studies. Berkshire still prints a sixty-year table of per-share book-value growth in every letter, letting anyone see the 19-plus percent compound rate since 1965.[2] In the UK, scientific-instrument roll-up Judges Scientific tracks the post-acquisition "Return on Total Invested Capital" for every deal and keeps that figure above 15 percent, year after year.[3]

2. Incentives That Mirror Ownership

Decentralized holdcos give operating CEOs wide autonomy and bonus them on cash returns on the capital they control. Equity options at head-office are minimal; real cash tied to subsidiary ROIC is what moves behavior. That keeps decision-making close to customers, caps bureaucracy, and protects margins when growth slows.

3. The Mathematics of Patience

Compound 15 percent and you triple capital in eight years; compound 25 percent and you triple it in five. Stretch that to twenty-five years and the gap widens to 33x versus 87x. Investors therefore accept a modest starting yield if management can recycle cash at >15 percent ROIIC for decades.

How Professionals Really Value a Holdco

Traditional multiples can mislead: Quality compounders often look expensive on EV/EBITDA. Instead of only looking at the traditional multiples, sophisticated buyers add the current FCF yield to the share of that cash that can be redeployed at attractive incremental returns. If that blended rate clears their required return (often 12 to 15 percent), they hold, sometimes for life.

- Berkshire Hathaway's 2024 free cash flow was roughly $11.6 billion ($30.6 billion operating cash flow less $19 billion capex) on a year-end market cap near $979 billion; a 1.2 percent base yield. If history repeats and about 70 percent of that cash is reinvested at ~15 percent ROIIC, the look-through return is roughly 11 percent.[4] At Berkshire's scale, an 11 percent look-through ROIIC is remarkable; few trillion-dollar firms can reinvest so much capital at double-digit rates. It reflects Buffett's rare ability to convert a modest cash yield into sustained, high-quality compounding through disciplined capital allocation.

- Constellation Software hit $1.47 billion in free cash flow available to shareholders in 2024. On a $65.5 billion market cap, this meant it was at about 2.2 percent. Management typically redeploys virtually every dollar at returns north of 25 percent, giving owners a blended return near 27 percent.[5] At that scale, a 27 percent look-through return is extraordinary, reflecting one of the most efficient capital allocation engines ever built. By continually redeploying nearly all free cash flow into hundreds of small, high-return acquisitions, Constellation sustains private-equity-like returns within a public company structure.
- Roper Technologies's free cash flow of $2.28 billion on a $53.8 billion market cap produced a 4.2 percent yield. Roper historically reinvests roughly 80 percent of cash at mid-teens returns, implying a 16 percent look-through rate—respectable for a mature industrial-tech compounder.[6]

Red-Flag Checklist

- **Leverage drift:** When net debt creeps above ~3x EBITDA without a visible plan to reduce it, interest costs start crowding out reinvestment and flexibility. The danger isn't just the headline number, but the behavior it signals, namely management shifting from disciplined compounding to financial engineering. Watch for rising acquisition sizes, slowing organic growth, or a shift from cash to mostly debt-funded deals.

- **Culture dilution:** When acquisition volume exceeds the organization's capacity to absorb and align new teams, clarity and accountability start to fray. Whether the model is centralized or decentralized, each addition still needs defined goals, reporting norms, and incentive alignment. Without deliberate onboarding and clear boundaries, the portfolio can drift into inconsistency—decisions slow, autonomy gets muddled, and the compounding engine loses the spark that kept it going.
- **Succession risk:** Compounding depends on continuity, not just of ownership, but of judgment. A holdco's greatest threat is a break in the chain of capable capital allocators who understand how to reinvest with discipline. A robust succession plan grooms future stewards early, exposing them to deal evaluation, capital budgeting, and incentive design long before they inherit authority. The goal is to preserve the firm's investing temperament across generations so that the compounding engine never stalls when leadership turns over.

When any two of these flash red, even tolerant shareholders should re-rate the company.

Behind every capital decision is a capital structure. Next, we'll break down how the best holdcos fund growth, contain risk, and build alignment into their governance.

VII

Capital Structure and Governance Foundations

Capital allocation is only as effective as the financial and governance architecture supporting it. The best holding companies don't just chase returns; they build durable structures that can absorb shocks, adapt to new environments, and endure across generations. Across the most successful holdcos, five foundational principles appear time and again.

1. Match Funding to Asset Durability

The nature of the underlying cash flows should dictate how a holdco funds itself. Long-dated, stable assets support higher leverage; short-term or volatile assets demand conservatism.

- Illinois Tool Works (ITW), a century-old industrial company, can safely carry 1–2x net debt/EBITDA because of the steady, predictable nature of its business.[1] It owns a diversified portfolio of industrial products sold to other businesses, many of which generate recurring demand. These stable cash flows allow ITW to take on moderate debt without risking liquidity. To further reduce risk, it staggers

its debt maturities over time to avoid large refinancing needs in any single year.[2]
- Constellation Software, which acquires small vertical-market software firms, is a study in contrast. Despite reliable cash flows, it has historically operated with modest leverage and often relies on seller financing and internal cash generation, which helps maintain flexibility if organic trends soften.[3] Vendor take-backs (where sellers finance part of the deal and are repaid over time) are common across CSI transactions.[4]
- Berkshire Hathaway pioneered perhaps the most elegant solution: *turning liabilities into assets*. Its insurance float, largely short-tail (insurance where claims are reported and settled quickly, as in home and auto insurance), becomes a de facto source of permanent capital—but only because Berkshire maintains world-class underwriting discipline.[5] GEICO and National Indemnity have produced sustained underwriting profits rather than losses, which allows the float to compound inside investments over long periods.[6]
- Danaher and Roper Technologies match long-duration industrial or SaaS-like assets with moderate leverage, continually adjusting debt profiles to acquisition cadence and asset reliability.[7,8]
- Brookfield matches long-term real assets (for example, infrastructure concessions) with long-dated, mostly non-recourse, fixed-rate debt and perpetual equity—that is, permanent capital from listed partnerships and evergreen funds with no requirement to return investor capital—allowing it to hold assets for decades and compound steadily over time.[9]

The lesson: Duration mismatch is one of the easiest ways to destroy a holding company. The best ones never forget this fact.

Note: Agencies present a unique challenge in matching liabilities to assets. Even retainer revenue is typically short-duration and cancellable, making cash flows less durable than in industrials or infrastructure. Since the core assets are people and client relationships and not long-lived or financeable, agency holdcos should avoid long-term debt and favor short-term, flexible credit to manage working capital. Acquisitions are best structured with seller notes or earn-outs tied to performance.

Public agency networks like WPP, Omnicom, and Interpublic typically maintain modest net leverage, rarely exceeding 2x EBITDA even with thousands of clients across global markets.[10] Smaller or mid-sized agencies, with less diversification, should be even more conservative. The most resilient agency groups maintain low leverage, ample liquidity, and governance structures that reflect the fragility of their revenue and the mobility of their talent.

2. Ring-Fence Risk

Great holdcos contain risk structurally. They isolate liabilities and insulate healthy businesses from troubled ones.

- Brookfield Asset Management pioneered the "listed partnership" model. If Brookfield Renewable or Brookfield Infrastructure encounters trouble, the parent BAM is shielded. Operating entities raise their own project-level debt and are structured as non-recourse entities.[11]
- Graham Holdings (formerly the Washington Post Co.) holds diverse assets in separate subsidiaries. During periods of regulatory scrutiny and write-downs at Kaplan's higher-education unit in 2010–2015, the company's other subsidiaries continued operating independently, illustrating the benefits of subsidiary-level separation.[12]

- Many lower middle-market holdcos—for example, Permanent Equity—are meticulous about placing seller notes and operating debt at the operating-company level, not at the parent level, which prevents contagion and preserves optionality.[13]

A ring-fenced structure lets the parent make bold bets without existential risk. It also protects the holdco's ability to continue compounding even if a single company falters.

3. Use the Cheapest *Stable* Capital First

Capital hierarchy isn't just about cost. It's about *stability under pressure*.

- Constellation Software often leans on seller financing and internally generated cash to fund acquisitions, which aligns outflows with performance and reduces reliance on third-party lenders. Heavy use of external debt can introduce covenants, refinancing risk, and pressure to maintain short-term earnings, all of which conflict with Constellation's patient, decentralized model. By contrast, funding growth from sellers and free cash flow preserves flexibility, keeps incentives aligned, and protects compounding through downturns.[14]
- HEICO, a disciplined compounder in aerospace, has long favored internally generated cash and low leverage, keeping balance-sheet risk modest relative to cash flow.[15]
- TransDigm goes the other way, aggressively using leveraged loans and high-yield debt to fund acquisitions. But it's calculated: The company's aftermarket aerospace parts have near-monopoly pricing and recurring demand. The

business can handle leverage because the cash flows are so robust and contractual.[16]

Most disciplined holdcos avoid floating-rate debt—loans whose interest costs rise automatically when central banks hike rates. What looks cheap in good times can become crippling in a tightening cycle, when borrowing costs climb and cash flow gets squeezed. Instead, these firms lock in fixed-rate debt with staggered maturities (a "ladder"), so only a small portion comes due at once, and they keep ample cash or unused credit lines on hand. The goal is simple: Never be forced into bad decisions just because the cost of money suddenly spikes.

4. Codify a Distribution Hierarchy

In the absence of a written plan, capital often flows to where it *feels good*: dividends, share buybacks, headline-grabbing acquisitions. But for long-term success, compounders must enforce discipline:

1. **Reinvest internally** at or above a hurdle rate (e.g., 15% ROIIC).
2. **Deleverage** to stay within target leverage bands.
3. **Repurchase shares** only when intrinsic value exceeds market price by 30%.
4. **Distribute dividends** with the residual cash.

Examples of this in practice:

- 3M pioneered this model in the postwar era, tying divisional autonomy to strict capital return criteria. While the system has since lost discipline, it influenced generations of industrial holdcos, including Roper and Fortive.

- Danaher's *Danaher Business System* (DBS) playbook includes investment hurdles, ROI screens, and post-acquisition reviews baked into its operating cadence. Every division must justify capital use against a standard return threshold, making decentralization effective without being chaotic.[17]
- Markel Group explicitly prioritizes reinvestment over dividends, believing that "great underwriting plus great investing beats capital return."[18]

A written distribution hierarchy protects against pressure to chase short-term investor sentiment and aligns the team to long-term value creation.

5. Govern Through Transparency and Alignment

No capital structure is complete without a governance backbone to keep incentives clean and decisions rational (more on this in the next chapter).

- Berkshire Hathaway's board includes capital allocators who think in decades. The annual letters, while informal in tone, function as an owner's manual. Buffett and Charlie Munger eschewed stock-based incentives and kept salaries nominal, so their wealth rose with Berkshire's intrinsic value rather than with grants.[19]
- Constellation Software ties bonuses primarily to organic growth and ROIC metrics; compensation is not tied to the stock price.[20]
- Danaher institutionalized the DBS, a process and culture so powerful it survives leadership transitions and has become the backbone of their governance. DBS is both a way of operating and a form of internal accountability.

The best holdcos operationalize culture through:

- Documented hurdle rates and decision memos.
- Acquisition tracking by deal year to evaluate long-term performance.
- Transparent incentive structures.
- Owner letters that double as operating handbooks.

You'll know governance is working when team members join not for perks or pay, but because they've read the letters and want to be part of the compounding.

A Note on Taxes for Holdcos

The following is meant to be educational only. This is not tax or legal advice. Confirm with qualified advisors.

Why it Belongs in Capital Structure and Governance

Taxes affect how you fund growth, ring-fence risk, and align behavior. They change how much cash survives each year, how easily you can move it to the parent, and how quickly the system compounds. For definitions and cash-flow mechanics, see the FCF formula in Chapter IV and the Bucket Group example in Chapter V.

Parent Form:

- **Pass-through parent (LLC or S corp).** Income flows to owners each year. It's simple and transparent, but owners owe current-year tax even when cash is retained for reinvestment.
- **C corp parent.** Tax is paid at the corporate level. The parent can retain and redeploy earnings before shareholder-level

tax, which can increase dollars available for allocation. Trade-off: potential double tax on distributions or certain exits.

Illustrative math (not advice): On $2.5 million of pre-tax income, a pass-through taxed at a high individual rate might retain about $1.575 million after tax; a C corp at the corporate rate might retain about $1.975 million. That is roughly $400,000 more per year to allocate. If just that incremental amount compounds at 15 percent for five years, it builds to about $2.7 million of additional parent capital. The point is deferral and reinvestment capacity, not that one form is always better.

How to decide: Match structure to behavior. Long holds and recycling favor corporate-level deferral; frequent asset sales or distributions often favor pass-throughs.

Group-Level Benefits a Holdco can Unlock

- **Consolidated group return.** If the parent is a U.S. C corp and owns at least 80 percent of each U.S. corporate subsidiary, you can file one federal tax return for the whole group. Dividends paid between group members are ignored on that return, so cash can usually move up to the parent with little extra tax.[21]

  Example: Opco A earns $1,000,000. Opco B loses $400,000. On a consolidated return, you pay tax on $600,000, not $1,000,000.

- **Intercompany dividends when you are not consolidated.** A U.S. corporate parent often receives a deduction for dividends from a U.S. corporate subsidiary, so moving cash up may create little or no tax at the parent.[22]

  Example: Opco pays a $1,000,000 dividend to the holdco. Because both are domestic C corps, the parent's taxable amount is reduced by the dividends-received deduction, so the tax on that upstreamed cash is small or zero. The later tax event for owners happens only if and when the parent pays a dividend to shareholders.

- **Where to put debt and losses.** Place borrowing within the entity that earns the income so interest deductions reduce that entity's taxable income, subject to interest-limitation rules.[23] Keep risky or experimental projects in their own subsidiaries to contain losses and simplify accounting.

  Example: You acquire a business and place the loan at the acquired company. Its interest expense reduces its taxable income there. You incubate a new product in a small subsidiary. If it fails, the loss sits in that entity and does not spill into lenders or unrelated operations.

- **State and local basics.** States have their own rules, and they do not always match the federal view. Two questions matter most:

  1. Where do we have to file? If you sell into a state or have employees in a state, you may owe tax there even without an office.[24]

  2. Who files together? Many states require combined or "unitary" reporting, which lumps related companies into one state return. That can help by letting losses offset profits, but it can also pull more income into a high-tax state.[24]

  Action items: Keep a one-page state map for every entity, note whether each state uses combined reporting, and document any intercompany management fees at arm's-length prices. Update the map after every acquisition.

  Example: You own a Texas distributor and a New York agency, but most customers are in California. California may tax a share of the group's income based on sales there, even if neither entity is headquartered in California.[25]

After-Tax Deal Outcomes

When you buy, sell, or reorganize, two levers drive the after-tax result:

- **Timing.** Some structures defer tax, which raises cash you can redeploy now.
- **Basis.** Some structures increase asset basis, creating future depreciation or amortization that lifts FCF later.

What to ask before signing a letter of intent (LOI):

Question	What it Really Means and What to Look For
Will this deal create an immediate tax bill or mostly defer it?	Some deal structures trigger taxes the moment you close, cutting into the cash you can reinvest. Others defer taxes until later, giving you more breathing room. Whenever possible, structure things so you can keep and reinvest the cash you just paid for. A small upfront tax can be fine if it makes the deal cleaner or cheaper.
Will we get new tax deductions from the purchase ("step-up in basis")?	A step-up lets you deduct more over time—like depreciation on equipment or software—freeing up extra cash each year. Ask your accountant to estimate how big those deductions could be and over how many years. If the seller resists, you might trade them a slightly higher price in exchange for getting those long-term benefits.
Where will the cash go after we close, and can we move it up to the parent easily?	Cash often gets stuck in the acquired company because of taxes, bank rules, or ownership structure. Ideally, you want a setup where you can move money freely—through dividends, management fees, or loans—to fund other parts of the business. It's okay if the cash stays put for a while, as long as it's earning a solid return there.

How will state or local taxes affect this setup?	Expanding into new states or regions can create surprise tax bills. Make sure your accountant maps where sales actually happen versus where entities are registered. Simpler structures, where operations and taxes line up, make life easier. Small inefficiencies are fine if they support strategic growth.
If we plan to hold the business, not flip it, will this deal design make cash flow stronger over the next few years?	Some deals look great on paper at closing but quietly hurt cash flow later—say, through high interest payments or earn-outs. Focus on how the business performs in years two to five, not just on day one. If you're buying to hold long term, prioritize steady, growing free cash flow over cosmetic short-term wins.

Moving Cash Inside the Group

- **Dividends vs. management fees.** Use dividends to move excess profits from C corp subsidiaries to the parent, especially if you file a consolidated return or the parent qualifies for a dividends deduction.

    Use a management fee only when the parent or a separate management company provides real services, like finance, HR, recruiting, IT, or marketing support. Fees must be arm's-length: define the scope, choose a reasonable pricing method, document the work, and invoice on normal terms.

    Some groups use a separate LLC or S corp management company owned by the principals to house shared services. This can be clean administratively, and the holdco's fee is deductible for those services, but it does not magically erase tax. It works best when the services are substantial and ongoing, and when payroll, state filings, and documentation are handled with care.

- **Keep ring-fencing.** Maintain legal separation and avoid parent guarantees unless necessary so a setback at one company cannot endanger the system as a whole.

Where Taxes Often Matter by Sector

- **Real estate.** Certain "like-kind exchange" rules allow real-estate owners to sell a property and roll the proceeds into another one without paying tax immediately. If the replacement is bought within specific time limits and debt levels are matched, your equity keeps compounding instead of being reduced by taxes. Think of it as swapping one property for another while keeping your investment dollars working.[27]

- **Agencies and other professional services.** Owners of pass-through entities (LLCs, S corps) pay tax each year on the profits their firms earn—even if they keep those profits inside the business. Once income passes a certain level, key deductions phase out and effective tax rates rise. In contrast, a C corp parent can defer tax at the owner level until profits are distributed as dividends or realized in a sale. If you plan to sell portfolio companies periodically rather than hold them long term, pass-through subsidiaries can be more efficient because they avoid a second layer of tax at the corporate level when you exit.

- **Product or software subsidiaries.** Early-stage C corps may qualify for a powerful incentive called the Qualified Small Business Stock (QSBS) exemption, under Section 1202 of the U.S. tax code. If the stock meets eligibility rules and is held for at least five years, shareholders can exclude up to 100 percent of the capital gain from federal tax when they sell. To qualify, the company must issue original stock when its assets are under $50 million and operate an active business—not simply hold investments or real estate. If there's a chance a subsidiary could meet these conditions, it's worth setting up cleanly from the start: Incorporate as a C corp, maintain proper records, and avoid activities that would disqualify the exemption.[28]

These are some things to look out for. Your situation and jurisdiction will determine what applies and what doesn't, so be sure to consult a tax professional.

Practical Guardrails

- Write a one-page tax architecture memo that states parent form, consolidation policy, how cash moves, intercompany pricing policy, a state filing matrix, and the annual review cadence.
- Before signing an LOI, ask for a one-page tax path: stock or asset, any basis step-up, how proceeds flow, expected immediate cash taxes, and required elections.
- Within ninety days post-close, run a tax audit: Confirm elections, map depreciable and amortizable basis, test interest-limitation exposure, and align intercompany agreements.
- Revisit parent form if behavior changes. Long holds and cash recycling favor deferral; frequent asset sales favor pass-throughs.

Bottom Line

The way you structure the group affects how cash is taxed. Taxes, in turn, affect compounding. Use your group architecture to reduce tax drag, retain earnings where behavior supports it, and create future tax deductions you can write off over time. Keep the structure simple, well documented, and aligned with the capital structure and governance discipline outlined in this chapter.

VIII

Compensation and Incentive Structures in Opco and Holdco Leadership

In holding company structures, effective compensation isn't merely a cost—it's a strategic lever that aligns operating company (opco) leaders with holdco objectives. This chapter explores best practices, frameworks, and practical examples to structure incentives that drive durable value creation by aligning these objectives.

The Importance of Aligned Incentives

Holding companies succeed when opco leaders act like owners, focusing on long-term capital allocation discipline and operational excellence. Misaligned incentives can lead to short-term thinking, inefficiencies, and conflicts. Well-structured incentives encourage leaders to make decisions aligned with the enduring success of the holdco.

Key Principles of Effective Compensation Structures

1. Long-Term Alignment:

Compensation should reward metrics reflecting sustainable value creation, such as free cash flow (FCF) growth, return on invested capital (ROIC), and return on incremental invested capital (ROIIC).

2. Simplicity and Transparency:

Incentive plans must be easily understandable, clearly measurable, and resistant to manipulation, reinforcing positive behaviors beneficial to the holdco.

3. Balanced Risk and Reward:

Encourage prudent decision-making that balances ambitious growth objectives with appropriate risk management.

Long-Term Incentive Plans (LTIPs): Equity and Equity-Like Alternatives

LTIPs create alignment between opco executives and the broader financial success of the holdco. Beyond cash bonuses, these plans offer meaningful incentives tied directly to equity value appreciation. Here are several common approaches:

1. Restricted Stock and Restricted Stock Units (RSUs):

Actual shares or share equivalents issued to executives, typically subject to vesting over three to five years, with vesting conditions based on time and/or performance milestones.

- **Realizing Value:** In public holdcos, vested RSUs become tradeable shares. In private holdcos, executives realize value through share repurchases by the holdco or structured secondary sales.

2. Stock Options:

Executives have the right, but not the obligation, to purchase shares at a predetermined "strike price," typically the fair market value at the grant date. Value accrues when the company's equity appreciates.

- **Realizing Value:** Public market sales or, if private, periodic buyback windows, secondaries, or a liquidity event (e.g., acquisition or IPO).

3. Phantom Stock and Stock Appreciation Rights (SARs):

No shares are actually granted; rather, executives receive cash payments tied directly to the appreciation of the holdco's equity value.

- **Realizing Value:** Cash payouts from holdco based on defined events (e.g., annual valuation, liquidity events, or vesting timelines).

4. Profits Interests (Common in LLCs and Partnerships):

Ownership units that grant a share of future appreciation (profits), but typically no immediate capital interest. These are often tax-efficient.

- **Realizing Value:** Distribution of profits or via secondary transactions, buybacks, or liquidity events.

5. Performance Shares:

Shares or share-equivalents awarded upon achieving predetermined financial targets (e.g., cumulative EBITDA growth, specific ROIC hurdles).

- **Realizing Value:** Similar mechanisms as RSUs (market sales, buybacks, liquidity events).

Realizing Equity Value: Public Markets, Secondaries, and Buybacks

How opco executives ultimately realize equity value depends significantly on whether the holdco is public or private.

Publicly Traded Holdcos:

- Executives typically realize equity value through public market transactions.
- Regular liquidity events occur as shares vest, with executives free to sell in the open market.

Privately Held Holdcos:

Private holdcos often establish structured liquidity mechanisms to help executives monetize equity incentives, including:

1. **Internal Buybacks:**

    Holdcos periodically offer to repurchase vested shares at fair market valuation. These typically occur annually or biennially, based on independent valuations or predetermined valuation formulas (e.g., 5x on trailing twelve-month EBITDA).

2. **Secondary Sales:**

    Privately negotiated transactions where executives sell vested shares to outside investors or back to the holdco in structured secondary rounds.

3. **Liquidity Events:**

    Ultimate liquidity often occurs through a strategic acquisition, merger, recapitalization, or IPO. LTIPs often explicitly address executive payouts in these scenarios.

Example of Opco Leader Incentive Structure: Bucket Group

Let's illustrate with Bucket Group, the holding company from the previous case study:

Bucket Group Opcos:
- Canister Agency: EBITDA $1.2M
- Pail Plumbing: EBITDA $800k
- Crate LMS: EBITDA $500k
- **Total Portfolio EBITDA:** $2.5M
- **Distributed Free Cash Flow:** $1.42M annually

Incentive Example for Canister Agency Leader:
Base Compensation:
- Annual Base Salary: $180,000

Annual Cash Bonus:
- Based on 10% of opco free cash flow contribution to holdco.
- Example: If Canister distributes $680k FCF, the annual bonus is $68,000.

Long-Term Equity Incentives:
- Canister CEO granted RSUs equal to 1% of holdco equity, vesting evenly over four years.
- Current holdco valuation: $8M. Thus, the CEO's initial grant value: $80,000.
- After four years, if Bucket Group valuation rises to $16M, vested RSUs are worth $160,000.

Realizing Value (Private Holdco Scenario):

Bucket Group periodically (every two years) buys back shares from executives at independently appraised market value. Executives have clear visibility into liquidity timelines.

- Initial RSU grant (1%): valued at $80,000 (at $8M valuation).
- After four years, Bucket Group's valuation is $16M.
- CEO sells vested 1% stake back to holdco in scheduled buyback, receiving a cash payout of $160,000.

Total Compensation Summary (over four years):

- Base salary: 4 x $180k = $720k
- Annual bonuses: 4 x $68k = $272k
- RSU buyback value after year four: $160k

Four-Year Total: $1,152,000

This illustrates powerful alignment: Executives profit meaningfully as the holdco equity value grows sustainably.

Structuring Holdco Leadership Compensation

At the holdco level, compensation typically emphasizes portfolio-wide performance metrics. Common metrics include:

- Aggregate free cash flow per share (FCF/share) growth.
- Portfolio-wide return on incremental invested capital (ROIIC) and return on invested capital (ROIC).
- Success rate and quality of acquisition integration.

Holdco leadership incentives generally mirror opco compensation structures, but offer larger equity or equity-like stakes (often 2 to 5 percent), vested according to multi-year portfolio performance milestones.

Example Executive Leader Compensation: Bucket Group

Let's illustrate with Bucket Group again:

Bucket Group Holdco (Year One):
- Total portfolio EBITDA: $2.5M
- Distributed free cash flow (FCF): $1.42M annually
- Initial holdco equity valuation: $8M (net of debt)

Incentive Example for Holdco Partner:

Base Compensation:
- Annual Base Salary: $225,000

Annual Cash Bonus:
- Based on achieving annual FCF/share growth above 10%.
- Example: If annual FCF/share grows by 12%, the bonus is 15% of annual salary.
- Annual Bonus: $225,000 x 15% = **$33,750**

Long-Term Equity Incentives:
- Holdco partner granted RSUs (or phantom equity) equal to 2.5% of holdco equity, vesting evenly over three years.
- Current holdco valuation: $8M. Thus, initial grant value is $8M x 2.5% = **$200,000** (approximately $66,667 per year vesting).
- After three years, if Bucket Group valuation rises to $15M, vested RSUs (2.5%) are worth: $15M x 2.5% = **$375,000**.

Realizing Value (Private Holdco Scenario):
- Bucket Group periodically (every two years) buys back shares from executives at independently appraised market value.
- Executives have clear visibility into liquidity timelines.
- Initial RSU grant (2.5%): valued at $200,000 at $8M valuation.
- After three years, holdco valuation is $15M.
- Holdco partner elects to sell half of vested equity (1.25%) back to holdco in scheduled buyback, receiving a cash payout of: $15M x 1.25% = **$187,500**.

Total Compensation Summary (over three years):
- Base Salary: 3 x $225k = **$675,000**
- Annual Bonuses: 3 x $33,750 = **$101,250**
- RSU buyback value after year three (partial stake): **$187,500**

Three-Year Total: $963,750

This illustrates powerful alignment: Holdco executive partners profit meaningfully as the holdco's portfolio value grows sustainably, rewarding disciplined capital allocation and long-term value creation.

Best Practices from Successful Holdcos

Successful holdcos carefully structure equity incentives, balancing meaningful participation with minimal dilution.

- At Constellation Software, senior executives are required to invest 75 percent of their after-tax annual incentive bonus into Constellation common shares, typically purchased on the open market and held under resale restrictions. The program focuses executives on ROIC and revenue growth while avoiding dilution from new equity grants.[1]

- At Danaher, equity incentives are structured around rigorous operational benchmarks and sustained performance. Danaher's executive compensation plans heavily emphasize performance-based vesting tied explicitly to operating and financial metrics, ensuring alignment with enduring shareholder value.[2]

- Buffett and Munger have strongly opposed stock-based compensation for Berkshire Hathaway executives in the past, arguing that it typically dilutes value and misaligns incentives. Berkshire managers receive cash bonuses directly tied to the clear operational performance of their individual business units. Managers who wish to own equity are encouraged, but not obligated, to buy Berkshire shares personally, using their own funds at market value. This ensures true alignment and preserves shareholder value.[3]

- StoicLane employs a clear and ambitious incentive structure, targeting a sustained 5x multiple on invested capital (MOIC) over three consecutive years. This ensures incentives reward durable, not temporary, value creation. All employees and sellers receive equity, further aligning stakeholder interests. As a private holding company, StoicLane provides structured liquidity via internal buybacks, secondary sales, or event-driven liquidity (e.g., recapitalization). This approach reinforces patient capital allocation and operational discipline, ensuring long-term alignment with holdco success.[4]

These approaches exemplify how thoughtful compensation structures, clearly tied to business outcomes and direct shareholder alignment, drive sustained and durable holdco value creation.

Summary: Compensation as a Strategic Lever

Clearly structured LTIPs, thoughtfully matched with business outcomes, are fundamental to creating sustained, long-term alignment. Incentives like RSUs, phantom stock, options, profits interests, and structured buybacks provide flexibility to tailor incentives to opco leadership. Ultimately, an effective compensation approach fosters ownership mindsets, disciplined capital allocation, and alignment of executive interests with enduring holdco value creation.

IX

When Holdcos Fail: Patterns, Signals, and Lessons

Holdcos rarely implode overnight. They erode quietly, then fail suddenly, usually after core disciplines have been abandoned. Across sectors and cycles, four failure patterns recur with near-religious regularity. Each tells a cautionary tale about what happens when the flywheel runs in reverse.

1. Leverage Outruns Cash

Tyco International became a symbol of inorganic bloat in the early 2000s. Under CEO Dennis Kozlowski, the company pursued hundreds of acquisitions across healthcare, electronics, and security. From 1999 through 2002, Tyco completed deals totaling about $40.4 billion in value.[1] The spree leaned on debt: By September 30, 2002, total debt stood at roughly $24.2 billion, with net debt around $18.0 billion.[2] When credit markets tightened, cash generation could not comfortably service obligations. Tyco restated financials and later faced SEC civil charges over disclosure and accounting issues.[3] Shares fell from about $60 in January 2002 to roughly $18 by December 2002.[4]

The lesson wasn't just about overleverage; it was about misunderstanding capital velocity. Even strong operating margins can't outrun the gravitational pull of compounding interest payments and goodwill impairment if the underlying assets aren't cash generative.

2. Incentives Distort Decisions

Valeant Pharmaceuticals (later Bausch Health) is a modern example of misaligned incentives at scale. Executive bonuses were heavily tied to revenue growth and "cash EPS," a non-GAAP measure the company highlighted in investor communications and used in annual incentive plans.[5] Valeant's acquisition engine bought growth and relied on price increases to boost earnings, but returns on invested capital deteriorated into 2015–2016.[6] The market concluded that Valeant was engineering earnings more than building durable value. The stock, which peaked above $260 in August 2015, traded below $10 by April 2017.[7]

As Charlie Munger put it: "Show me the incentive, and I'll show you the outcome." In Valeant's case, executives were paid handsomely to mortgage the company's future for short-term optics.

3. Culture Smothers Autonomy

Thrasio, the once-vaunted Amazon FBA aggregator, was founded on a seductive idea: Roll up thousands of profitable third-party seller businesses and apply centralized best practices to scale them efficiently. The thesis made sense on paper: margin expansion via cost savings, advertising synergies, and supply chain leverage.

Integration proved far messier in practice. By 2022, the company announced significant layoffs and a CEO transition as it tried to right-size the organization.[8] Thrasio filed for Chapter 11 in February

2024 and emerged in June 2024; Stephanie Fox, previously COO, was appointed CEO to focus on profitability after restructuring.[9,10] What started as a decentralized bet on operational excellence became a centralized tangle of half-integrated assets and strained systems.

The deeper failure wasn't just operational, but philosophical. Autonomy, the core advantage of a decentralized holdco, only works when backed by scalable systems, trust in local operators, and a clear culture of ownership. Thrasio tried to own the businesses without empowering the people who ran them.

4. Growth Narrative Eclipses Cash Economics

GE Capital believed that financial engineering could replace industrial cash flow. On paper, it was a star, producing more than half of GE's total profits by 2007.[11] But much of those "profits" came from financial assets that accelerated accounting income while cash showed up more slowly. Meanwhile, GE returned large sums to shareholders and funded acquisitions, deepening reliance on short-term funding.

When the 2008 crisis froze credit markets, GE's dependence on commercial paper and short-term debt became a liability; at year-end, GE Capital had over $100 billion of commercial paper outstanding and ran at roughly 8.1:1 debt-to-equity.[12] In late 2008, GE turned to government backstops to keep funding lines open. It borrowed through the Federal Reserve's Commercial Paper Funding Facility and issued medium-term notes guaranteed by the FDIC under the Temporary Liquidity Guarantee Program, moves that stabilized liquidity but underscored the fragility of its balance sheet. These steps marked the beginning of a multi-year restructuring of GE Capital.[13,14]

Modern echoes of this story can be found in the era of special-purpose acquisition companies (SPACs) conducting roll-ups that pay 20–30x EBITDA for pre-profit consumer brands or low-margin logistics networks, betting that scale alone would solve for cash. But few things are as unforgiving as poor cash economics disguised by a growth story.

Early Warning Signals: What to Watch

These warning signs rarely scream; they whisper. But when multiple signs flash at once, the compounding engine may be in reverse. Watch out for the following warning signs:

- Free cash flow per share growth lags inflation for two or more years.
    - Your reinvestment strategy may be stalling, masked by financial optics.
- Net debt/EBITDA exceeds 3x and keeps rising.
    - Debt, not operations, is fueling perceived value creation.
- New acquisition vintages earn ROIIC below the firm's weighted average cost of capital (WACC).
    - You are destroying long-term value with every dollar spent.
- Selling, general, and administrative expenses (SG&A) as a percent of revenue balloons post-acquisition.
    - The added costs of integration are wiping out the expected synergies.
- Senior operator turnover exceeds 20 percent within two years of acquisition.
    - Your cultural model is failing to attract or retain entrepreneurial talent.

Case-Study Takeaways

- Tyco: Growth that is funded by leverage is a ticking clock. Even assets with 40 percent or more returns on capital can be sunk by a capital structure that collapses under pressure.
- Valeant: Incentives create gravity. If you tie pay to manipulated metrics, the business will drift toward fragility.
- Thrasio: Systems and autonomy must evolve in lockstep. Scaling without upgrading operating infrastructure is like driving a Formula 1 car on dirt roads.
- GE Capital: Earnings that don't convert to cash are mirages. And the bigger the mirage, the harder the crash when reality intrudes.

Bottom line: Holding companies succeed or fail not because of their ideas, but because of their habits. The ones that endure institutionalize patience, transparency, and cash discipline. The ones that don't usually look brilliant … right until they break.

X

Build a Holdco Workshop

Now that you've been exposed to core holdco concepts, let's try our hand at sketching one out. The following exercise is designed to help prospective holdco builders sketch a clear, narrative-driven blueprint before getting tangled in spreadsheets or deal models. The goal is to develop conviction around three foundational questions:

1. What business arenas will we play in?
2. What kinds of companies will we own?
3. How will cash reliably flow from our opcos to the parent, and back into growth?

This is not about optimization; it's about sharpening intent. Optimization comes later, when you have real numbers, constraints, and opportunities to refine. But without intent—clarity of purpose, investment philosophy, and design principles—you risk building a collection of assets rather than a coherent system. Intent defines what good looks like before you ever touch a model.

Step 1: Start with the playing field.

List two to four industries where you have enough understanding to spot above-average operators, pricing power, or overlooked market structures.

Generic ambition ("any profitable business") won't cut it. You're defining the sandbox in which you'll build long-term. Look for sectors with recurring customer needs, potential for operational improvement, and macro trends that provide tailwinds. Fragmented categories, where you can buy well at low multiples, often make better hunting grounds than buzzy spaces where people may tend to be overbidding.

Step 2: Define the shape of your ideal company.

Forget formulas for now. Focus on qualitative traits that signal when a business is worth owning.

- What kinds of moats do you prefer? Regulatory licenses, customer lock-in, route density, proprietary data?
- What is your stance on founder involvement? Will you retain them as minority partners or insert your own operator?
- What's your tolerance for complexity? How many SKUs, revenue lines, or team members before a business becomes operationally brittle?
- And culturally, will your holdco favor autonomy or enforce a tight playbook?

These answers will inform your entire approach to governance and incentives.

Step 3: Clarify your capital deployment philosophy.

Imagine you've just received a fresh dollar of free cash flow. Where does it go first? Will you reinvest inside the opco if the project clears a qualitative hurdle, such as margin expansion or access to a new niche? Will you prioritize bolt-on acquisitions? Or do you view the balance sheet itself as a compounding tool, using seller notes, debt, and non-recourse financing to stretch capital while protecting the core?

There's no right answer, only the one that reflects your temperament and strategy. Write it down. Your response will expose how you naturally weigh growth against safety, ownership concentration against diversification, and patience against speed.

Why it matters:

- Reveals your true risk posture. Are you a reinvestor who compounds internally, or an acquirer who compounds through deal flow?
- Clarifies your deployment cadence. How often do you expect to put capital to work—and under what conditions do you choose to hold back?
- Surfaces your bias toward leverage. Do you prefer stretching capital with debt or preserving flexibility with equity?
- Creates a reference point. Documenting this philosophy now allows you to revisit it later as your balance sheet, market, and confidence evolve.

Step 4: Visualize the cash flow pathway.

Sketch out how money will move through your system:

- What triggers a distribution from opco to holdco? E.g., when cash exceeds two months' payroll, or at quarterly intervals after debt service.
- At the parent level, what are the top two uses of that cash? Will you maintain dry powder for opportunistic acquisitions, invest in central capabilities, or pay down debt?
- Finally, under what conditions, if any, will cash be returned to owners? Articulate the rules now, in plain language, so the system doesn't drift later.

Step 5: Find your reference points and strategic fit.

Before finalizing your vision, revisit the holdco examples and sector-specific models outlined earlier in this guide and in the appendix. Which ones mirror your ambition? Are you closer to a focused agency roll-up, a decentralized industrial compounder, or a brand incubator with shared infrastructure?

Use these precedents to pressure-test your decisions around autonomy, capital flow, team structure, and sector scope. The goal isn't to copy a model, but to place your strategy on the map and sharpen where it diverges.

Step 6: Commit to a vision and write a one-pager.

Take everything you've outlined and distill it into a single paragraph, a fifty-word statement that could sit at the top of your investor memo or company site. If it sounds generic, you likely haven't gone deep enough in the earlier steps. Push for clarity. Make it sound like something only you could have written.

When you're done, you'll have a one-page conceptual playbook—a focused point of view that will inform deal sourcing, capital allocation, and org design from day one. The numbers will come later. This is where strategic clarity begins.

Example: Barrel Holdings Conceptual Playbook

1. **Playing Field**

    We focus on acquiring and growing specialized agencies. These are expert-driven firms that serve a specific vertical and/or function (e.g., Shopify ecommerce, Amazon advertising, WordPress maintenance) and often operate within fragmented, underserved markets. The agency model, when built on recurring or sticky client relationships and margin discipline, produces reliable cash flow. Our edge is in knowing how to help these firms grow profitably without compromising their craft and culture.

2. **Target Company Shape**

    We seek agencies that exhibit:
    - Deep specialization in a specific vertical, platform, channel, or service.
    - Strong client retention and low churn.
    - Twenty percent or more net margins with AI leverage or lean delivery models.
    - Founders who are looking for liquidity and strategic support, or who are ready to hand off reins to a strong leadership team.
    - Clear but untapped growth levers (pricing, packaging, sales process, cross-sell).

We favor companies where we can preserve team culture and autonomy while adding lift through various support services and accountability structures.

3. **Capital Deployment Philosophy**

   Agencies are expected to run lean, sending excess cash to the holdco. We centralize capital allocation, using upstreamed cash to fund acquisitions and build shared capabilities that benefit the entire portfolio. Owner distributions are secondary; our priority is long-term compounding through disciplined reinvestment.

4. **Cash Flow Pathway**

   Opcos retain modest reserves for stability, but excess cash flows to holdco quarterly. Agency leaders are incentivized to maximize upstream cash via profit share.

5. **Strategic Reference Points**

   Barrel Holdings blends the disciplined capital deployment of Constellation Software with the patient ownership mindset of Permanent Equity. We also take inspiration from the operational discipline of Danaher and their DBS, leveraging our own Agency Systems Playbook to help our agencies embrace best practices.

   We're focused on specialized agencies where long-term client relationships, operational leverage, and niche expertise can compound quietly over time. We avoid financial engineering, lean into operational discipline, and invest for durability.

6. **Vision Statement**

   Barrel Holdings is building a portfolio of high-margin, low-churn specialized agencies. Through focused acquisitions and smart reinvestment, we aim to create a long-lasting, cash-flowing company that supports talented teams and compounds value without sacrificing autonomy or quality.

Ready to put together your own holdco vision? Give it a go!

XI

Private Equity's Holdco Evolution

From Funds to Platforms: The Dual Nature of Private Equity

Private equity has long been anchored in the fund model. A PE fund is typically a closed-end investment vehicle, structured as a limited partnership, in which a general partner (GP) raises capital from institutional limited partners (LPs). The fund has a defined lifecycle (usually ten years), within which capital is deployed during the first half and harvested in the second. The GP's role is primarily financial: to identify opportunities, allocate capital across investments, and oversee performance with an eye toward maximizing returns within the fund's time horizon.

In contrast, what's often referred to as a "PE platform" introduces a different dynamic. Instead of acting as a pure capital allocator, the PE firm acquires or creates an operating company that serves as a foundation for bolt-on acquisitions. This platform company becomes an active business operator (often legally structured as a holding company), consolidating and managing a network of businesses. While still intended for eventual exit, the platform is designed to compound value operationally, not just financially.

In this way, the PE firm begins to play a dual role: financial sponsor at the fund level and business owner/operator at the platform level. This model bridges the traditional fund paradigm with the kind of operational control and compounding philosophy more commonly found in permanent capital vehicles.

The Rise of Permanent Capital and Holdco-Like Structures

Over the past decade, some of the most influential private equity firms have quietly been transforming themselves from fund managers into diversified, operator-led financial holding companies. The rise of permanent capital—capital that is not subject to the rigid constraints of fund lifecycles—has been a major catalyst in this shift.

Take KKR, for example. Once known primarily for its leveraged buyouts, KKR has become a publicly traded investment firm that not only manages funds but also owns businesses directly through its growing balance sheet. Its acquisition of Global Atlantic, a life and annuity insurance platform, gives it access to long-duration liabilities that provide a stable source of investable capital.[1] Rather than using the capital to invest directly as an owner, KKR manages these assets to generate fee income, essentially turning the insurer into a captive distribution channel for its credit and alternatives strategies.[2]

Apollo Global Management has followed a similar model through its merger with Athene in 2022.[3] Athene generates long-term liabilities by selling retirement and annuity products, and Apollo, in turn, manages the corresponding assets, often in yield-seeking strategies built in-house.[4] While the cash flows from Athene stabilize Apollo's earnings and grow its AUM, the insurance capital is treated as fee-generating fuel, not float to be invested directly for shareholders.

In this way, Apollo is not building a float-compounding engine like Berkshire Hathaway, but rather constructing a highly efficient, capital-light asset management platform with a recurring inflow of client capital.

This is a crucial distinction. Berkshire Hathaway owns its insurance subsidiaries outright and treats the float generated as permanent, cost-free capital. That float is not managed for fees; it is invested directly, with the full return accruing to Berkshire's shareholders. This gives Berkshire a structurally unique advantage: It can operate without the drag of third-party incentive structures, hold assets as long as it wishes, and compound capital across market cycles without pressure to exit.[5] In contrast, firms like Apollo and KKR use their insurance businesses primarily to scale their asset management operations. The result is higher fee-related earnings and greater scalability, but also a different alignment of incentives.

Ares Management, known originally for credit, has expanded via Ares-managed vehicles into infrastructure and operating assets, while its corporate model remains oriented around fee generation rather than balance-sheet investing.[6]

Blackstone, one of the largest alternative asset managers by AUM, has maintained a fee-oriented manager identity but built powerful capital ecosystems around real estate (BREIT) and credit and insurance (BXCI). These verticals are anchored by perpetual-capital vehicles that provide stability and recurring fees.[7]

Then there's Brookfield, which is arguably the most holdco-like. Structured through Brookfield Corporation and its publicly-listed asset management spinoff, Brookfield operates utilities, infrastructure, real estate, and private equity holdings with a long-term owner-operator mindset. Governance is led by operators, and many of its businesses are permanent fixtures, not portfolio companies waiting for exit.[8]

What This Means

At a glance, these firms still raise funds, charge management fees, and distribute carry. But peel back the structure, and it's clear they are shifting toward something more hybrid in nature:

- They invest directly off their own balance sheets.
- They build or acquire operating businesses.
- They generate recurring liabilities through insurance and infrastructure.
- They hold assets longer and harvest recurring fees, not just capital gains.

In doing so, they blur the lines between PE firms, holdcos, and asset managers. What emerges is a new breed of capital allocator: one that enjoys the capital access and scale of an asset manager, the control and duration of a holding company, and the optionality of a PE firm.

Still, there's a fundamental difference in how capital flows through the system. Firms like Apollo and KKR treat insurance as a means of gathering and managing capital for fees, whereas Berkshire treats insurance as a source of permanent capital to invest directly. Both models can be powerful; one is built to generate value through fee-based capital management, the other through long-term compounding of retained earnings.

For entrepreneurs and investors studying holdcos, this transformation reveals something important: Permanence, flexibility, and cash flow are not exclusive to Berkshire-style compounders. But how those advantages are captured and allocated, and who keeps the upside, varies widely depending on the model.

XII

Superacquirers

Superacquirers are companies that grow predominantly through acquisition, but unlike traditional holding companies, they don't keep those acquisitions independent. Instead, they fully absorb them, integrating brand, systems, people, and operations into a single unified structure. Over time, what began as a series of acquisitions starts to resemble one large, tightly run business rather than a portfolio of distinct companies.

This model favors centralization. Acquired companies are rebranded, often restructured, and expected to operate under common systems, processes, and leadership. The result is operational consistency, a unified customer experience, and the ability to scale quickly through repeatable integration playbooks.

While every company has its own flavor, superacquirers generally share the following traits:

- **One brand, many acquisitions:** New companies are rolled into a single corporate identity, dissolving legacy brands.
- **Centralized operations and leadership:** Decisions are driven from the top, with a strong emphasis on consistency and efficiency.

- **Unified tech and culture:** Core systems, tools, and values are standardized across the organization.
- **M&A as capability acquisition:** Deals are often pursued to add new competencies, geographies, or market segments that fit into the existing machine.

In contrast, traditional holdcos maintain the autonomy of their operating companies. Each entity has its own leadership, brand, and often its own way of doing business. This decentralization gives holdcos greater flexibility and resilience, but less cohesion. Superacquirers, by comparison, trade optionality for integration.

Superacquirers vs. Operational Holdcos

At first glance, superacquirers might resemble operational holding companies like Danaher, Fortive, or Roper Technologies, which also pursue M&A aggressively and are deeply involved in operations. But there's a crucial difference in how they preserve structure and value.

Operational holdcos, sometimes referred to as compounders, maintain modular autonomy at the business unit level. Their portfolio companies retain distinct identities, P&Ls, and often leadership teams, even as they are guided by a shared set of operating principles like the Danaher Business System. Integration is targeted and strategic, not totalizing.

Operational holdcos preserve boundaries. The acquired company joins the ecosystem but continues to function with a high degree of autonomy within that system. In contrast, superacquirers erase boundaries. The acquired company becomes part of the whole, and its independence is surrendered.

This distinction matters because it shapes:

- Cultural resilience: Operational holdcos tolerate (and even encourage) cultural diversity across business units. Superacquirers impose one dominant culture.
- Scalability vs. fragility: Superacquirers risk bloat and integration fatigue if acquisitions outpace their ability to harmonize. Operational holdcos can scale with less friction by isolating complexity in each unit.
- Capital allocation flexibility: Operational holdcos often deploy capital to the highest-performing units or to new acquisitions without disrupting the rest. Superacquirers treat the whole as one machine, making incremental optimization more difficult.

Many business leaders hear "acquisition-driven growth" and assume the mechanics are the same. But superacquirers and holdcos (traditional or operational) are playing very different games.

- Superacquirers are building scale through uniformity.
- Operational holdcos are building durability through diversity and discipline.

Knowing the difference is critical, whether you're selling your business, joining as an executive, or evaluating a potential investment. If you become part of a superacquirer, expect full assimilation. Your systems, brand, and perhaps your team will disappear into a larger structure. In an operational holdco, you may retain your identity but be expected to operate with rigor, discipline, and alignment to a proven playbook.

Real-World Superacquirer Examples

- Accenture has absorbed countless consulting and digital services firms into its global brand, building consistency across its offerings.[1]
- S4 Capital integrates marketing firms under its unified Monks banner, streamlining creative and data operations.[2]
- CGI Inc.,[3] Capgemini,[4] and Wipro[5] all follow a similar model in IT services—growing through acquisitions, then standardizing operations globally.

These firms don't think in terms of a portfolio. They think in terms of scale. Each acquisition is another cog in the machine; not a standalone business, but part of something larger and more tightly orchestrated.

Superacquirers and holdcos both rely on M&A, but what they're building and how they behave is fundamentally different. Superacquirers are integration machines; operational holdcos are systems of systems. Both can be highly successful, but the strategic, cultural, and financial implications diverge sharply.

For those building or backing acquisition-driven organizations, knowing which path you're on is the first step in deciding how to grow and how to lead.

XIII

Creator Holdcos and Personal Holdcos

Not all holding companies start with capital. Some begin with attention or a set of personal operating principles. In this chapter, we examine two emerging models: creator holdcos and personal holdcos. While both depart from traditional corporate origins, they reflect the same foundational behaviors: leveraging assets to create, fund, and compound multiple ventures over time.

Creator Holdcos

Creator holdcos emerge when individuals with large audiences—typically through YouTube, TikTok, podcasting, or legacy celebrity status—parlay their reach into ownership across multiple businesses. These aren't just licensing deals. Many creators now function as de facto capital allocators, spinning up or acquiring consumer brands, tech products, media companies, and even real estate assets.

Classic celebrity precedents include Shaquille O'Neal, who has ownership in fast food, fitness centers, and real estate;[1] George Clooney, whose Casamigos tequila sold for nearly $1B;[2] and Greg Norman, who built a diversified lifestyle brand across apparel, wine, and golf course design.[3] These were creator holdcos before the term existed. Today's influencers are following a similar path, but with direct digital access to fans and vastly lower distribution costs.

MrBeast (Jimmy Donaldson) is arguably the highest-profile example. Through Beast Holdings, he has built a portfolio including a snack brand (Feastables), a now-defunct virtual restaurant chain (MrBeast Burger), a mobile game, a content production arm, and even a creator analytics SaaS tool (ViewStats).[4] Beast Holdings reported $473 million in revenue in 2023 and projects over $800 million in 2025.[5] While impressive, most of these figures come from self-reporting or speculative investor decks. It's still unclear how much recurring profit is generated and how well each business performs without the halo of his brand.

The **Sidemen**, a British YouTube collective, have built a multi-brand empire through Sides (QSR chicken franchise), XIX Vodka, Sidemen Clothing, and a fan subscription business (Side+).[6] They recently launched an £18 million venture fund, positioning themselves as creator-led capital allocators.[7] Again, details on profitability or governance structure are limited, but the integrated approach resembles an operational holdco: shared content, cross-brand promotion, and repeat customer engagement.

These ventures often rely heavily on distribution, not operational excellence. Rarely do creator holdcos show signs of applying deliberate capital allocation frameworks, portfolio governance, or reinvestment hurdle rates. The playbook is more often to use brands to generate attention, attention to drive traffic, and traffic to monetize across owned products. This can create impressive cash surges, but may not translate into compounding value unless those surges are reinvested strategically.

Risk and sustainability remain open questions. Most creator holdcos are private, so we don't know cash flow margins, retention curves, or cost structures. Several high-profile ventures, such as

MrBeast Burger, Jake Paul's NFTs, or D'Amelio-backed brands have fizzled, been sold, or hit legal troubles. The churn rate is likely high. Distribution gets you in the door; only sound operating models and governance keep you there.

Still, the model is real. And from Emma Chamberlain's boutique coffee brand[8] to Marques Brownlee's media production company,[9] smaller creators are also building multi-asset platforms. In many cases, they bootstrap new ventures using profits from earlier businesses. Sahil Bloom, for example, has launched a newsletter, a YouTube channel, a marketing agency, a creator tech startup, and a venture fund, all linked through a central personal brand.[10] While not yet a traditional holdco, he's converging on the structure.

Personal Holdcos

If creator holdcos begin with audience, personal holdcos begin with mindset. This model treats the individual as the investor, CEO, and board with a focus on allocating capital, time, and energy across a portfolio of businesses, assets, and long-term bets.

At the extreme end is Elon Musk, whose control of Tesla, SpaceX, Neuralink, X (formerly Twitter), and xAI demonstrates a coherent (if idiosyncratic) capital allocation approach. Musk uses brand power, personal equity, and private capital to fund new ventures and cross-pollinate talent and IP. He moves cash and people between entities, raises against one to fund another, and orchestrates product rollouts across brands (e.g., Grok AI surfaced inside X via xAI).[11] While few can replicate this scale, the model (strategic control across multiple companies, driven by one allocator) is the clearest example of a personal holdco in action.

At smaller scales, Michael Karnjanaprakorn has advocated the personal holdco mindset explicitly. His post-venture studio Choop includes content, angel investments, service businesses, real estate, and product experiments. Karnjanaprakorn doesn't treat each project as a startup to scale and sell; instead, he's optimizing for optionality, lifestyle alignment, and long-term wealth creation.[12]

Michael Girdley runs a $100M-plus portfolio of twelve-plus companies across software, services, and consumer. He acts as capital allocator, board member, and systems enabler. His businesses are intentionally held, not flipped. Cash is reinvested into new acquisitions or talent, not siphoned off. Girdley emphasizes decentralized operations with centralized discipline, a classic holdco trait.[13]

Codie Sanchez popularized buying "boring businesses" (e.g., laundromats, car washes, vending routes) and turning them into compounding cash engines. Her Contrarian Thinking platform generates leads, recruits capital, and sells education products. These cash flows are then reinvested into acquiring more small businesses. While branded under media and education, her structure operates like a buy-and-hold micro PE firm, just with a broader audience and brand narrative amplifying it.[14]

Others, like Nick Huber, Yong-Soo Chung, and Shaan Puri, have taken different angles, combining real estate, SaaS, media, and services in bespoke portfolios. The common thread is control: They fund what they own, own what they operate, and redeploy profits into new ventures without institutional LPs or VC pressure.[15]

What makes a personal holdco distinct isn't the legal structure, but the behavior:

- Viewing each dollar as capital, not income
- Reinvesting excess cash into adjacent or synergistic projects
- Maintaining ownership and control
- Using systems and teams to free up the allocator's time

In many ways, the personal holdco is the most accessible model for entrepreneurs. It requires no audience, no investors—just discipline and a long view. Like any good holdco, it thrives on cash generation, reinvestment discipline, and optionality.

Creator and personal holdcos may look different on the surface—one driven by reach, the other by intentionality—but both reflect a common shift. Entrepreneurs are rejecting single-venture dependency in favor of diversified, self-directed portfolios. Some do it with distribution. Others do it with cash flow. The best do it with both, and compound over decades.

ENDNOTES

Chapter I: What is a Holding Company?
1. Berkshire Hathaway Inc., "2024 Annual Report," https://www.berkshirehathaway.com/2024ar/2024ar.pdf (accessed June 2025).
2. Danaher Corporation, "The Danaher Business System," https://www.danaher.com/how-we-work/danaher-business-system (accessed June 2025).
3. Trive Capital, "Investment Strategy & Criteria," https://www.trivecapital.com/strategy/ (accessed June 2025).

Chapter III: Sector-Specific Holding Companies
1. WPP plc, "Annual Report & Accounts 2024, Strategic Report," https://www.wpp.com/-/media/project/wpp/files/investors/2025/annual-report/wpp_annual_report_2024_strategic-report.pdf (accessed June 2025).
2. Stagwell Inc., "Network," https://www.stagwellglobal.com/network (accessed June 2025).
3. LVMH Moët Hennessy Louis Vuitton SE, "LVMH completes the acquisition of Tiffany & Co.," press release, U.S. SEC EDGAR Exhibit 99.1, January 7, 2021, https://www.sec.gov/Archives/edgar/data/98246/000119312521004213/d301758dex991.htm (accessed June 2025).

4. Church & Dwight Co., Inc., "2024 Annual Report," https://s203.q4cdn.com/233583214/files/doc_financials/2024/ar/Final-AR-for-website.pdf (accessed June 2025).
5. FirstService Corporation, "2024 Annual Report," https://www.firstservice.com/wp-content/uploads/2025/03/FirstService-Annual-Report-2024-WEB.pdf (accessed June 2025).
6. TurnPoint Services, "Home," https://www.turnpointservices.com (accessed June 2025).
7. ACHR News, "TurnPoint Services Completes 21 Acquisitions in 2021," January 18, 2022, https://www.achrnews.com/articles/146013-turnpoint-services-completes-21-acquisitions-in-2021 (accessed June 2025).
8. Constellation Software Inc., "Q4 2024 Shareholder Report," https://www.csisoftware.com/docs/default-source/press-releases/q4-2024-shareholder-report.pdf (accessed June 2025).
9. Constellation Software Inc., "Q3 2023 Shareholders' Report (MD&A)," acquisition structures including holdbacks and contingent consideration, https://www.csisoftware.com/docs/default-source/investor-relations/statutory-filings/csi---mda-q3-2023---final.pdf (accessed June 2025).
10. Colin Keeley, "ESW Capital Operating Manual: How an empire was built on 150+ software acquisitions and hardcore shared services," https://www.colinkeeley.com/blog/esw-capital-operating-manual (accessed June 2025).
11. Danaher Corporation, "The Danaher Business System," https://www.danaher.com/how-we-work/danaher-business-system (accessed June 2025).
12. Illinois Tool Works Inc., "Form 10-K 2024," https://s204.q4cdn.com/218186261/files/doc_financials/2025/sr/10-K.pdf (accessed June 2025).

13. Darden Restaurants, Inc., "Form 10-K 2024 with shareholder letter," https://s27.q4cdn.com/308865545/files/doc_financials/2024/ar/dri-fy24-10-k-with-shareholder-letter.pdf (accessed June 2025).
14. Restaurant Brands International Inc., "Form 10-K 2024," https://s26.q4cdn.com/317237604/files/doc_financials/2024/ar/b16f0901-feeb-4cff-9658-3baf738cef10.pdf (accessed June 2025).

Chapter VI: The Investor Lens: Why Multi-Decade Compounders Win

1. Warren E. Buffett, "Berkshire Hathaway Shareholder Letters," Berkshire Hathaway Inc., https://www.berkshirehathaway.com/letters/letters.html (accessed June 2025).
2. Warren E. Buffett, "Berkshire Hathaway Shareholder Letters," Berkshire Hathaway Inc., https://www.berkshirehathaway.com/letters/letters.html (accessed June 2025).
3. Judges Scientific plc, "Financial Reports," https://www.judges.uk.com/financial-performance/reports.html (accessed June 2025).
4. Berkshire Hathaway Inc., 2024 Annual Report (Omaha: Berkshire Hathaway, 2025).
5. Constellation Software Inc., "Constellation Software Inc. Announces Results for the Fourth Quarter and Year Ended December 31, 2024 and Declares Quarterly Dividend," press release, March 2025, https://www.csisoftware.com/category/press-releases (accessed June 2025).
6. Roper Technologies, Inc., Form 10-K 2024 (Sarasota, FL: Roper, 2025).

Chapter VII: Capital Structure and Governance Foundations

1. Illinois Tool Works Inc., "Form 10-K 2024," https://s204.q4cdn.com/218186261/files/doc_financials/2025/sr/10-K.pdf (accessed June 2025).
2. Illinois Tool Works Inc., "Form 10-K 2024," Note on borrowings and scheduled maturities of long-term debt, https://s204.q4cdn.com/218186261/files/doc_financials/2025/sr/10-K.pdf (accessed June 2025).
3. Constellation Software Inc., "Q4 2024 Shareholder Report," https://www.csisoftware.com/docs/default-source/press-releases/q4-2024-shareholder-report.pdf (accessed June 2025).
4. Constellation Software Inc., "Q3 2023 Shareholders' Report (MD&A)," acquisition structures including holdbacks and contingent consideration, https://www.csisoftware.com/docs/default-source/investor-relations/statutory-filings/csi---mda-q3-2023---final.pdf (accessed June 2025).
5. Berkshire Hathaway Inc., "2024 Annual Report," https://www.berkshirehathaway.com/2024ar/2024ar.pdf (accessed June 2025).
6. Berkshire Hathaway Inc., "2024 Annual Report," Insurance—Underwriting section, https://www.berkshirehathaway.com/2024ar/2024ar.pdf (accessed June 2025).
7. Danaher Corporation, "2024 Annual Report," https://filecache.investorroom.com/mr5ir_danaher/911/download/Danaher%202024%20Annual%20Report.pdf (accessed June 2025).
8. Roper Technologies, Inc., "Financial Results 2024," news release and investor materials, https://www.ropertech.com/news-releases/news-release-details/roper-technologies-announces-2024-financial-results (accessed June 2025).

9. Brookfield Renewable Partners, "2024 Annual Report," https://bep.brookfield.com/sites/bep-brookfield-ir/files/Brookfield-BEP-IR-V2/2025/bep-2024-annual-report.pdf (accessed June 2025).
10. WPP plc, "Annual Report 2024," https://www.wpp.com/-/media/project/wpp/files/investors/2025/annual-report/wpp_annual_report_2024.pdf (accessed June 2025); Omnicom Group Inc., "Q2 2025 Investor Presentation," https://s201.q4cdn.com/282904488/files/doc_financials/2025/q2/OMC-2025-Q2-Investor-Presentation-07-15-25-FINAL.pdf (accessed June 2025); Interpublic Group, investor materials on leverage ratios, https://investors.interpublic.com/static-files/3d16d498-bc26-411f-adb7-87fb67e9ad61 (accessed June 2025).
11. Brookfield Corporation, "Q3 2023 Letter to Shareholders," https://bn.brookfield.com/reports-filings/letters-shareholders/q3-2023-letter-to-shareholders (accessed June 2025).
12. Graham Holdings Company, Form 10-K (filed Feb. 26, 2025), diversified subsidiaries and segment structure, https://www.ghco.com/static-files/d43e6f46-dc9b-4822-857a-4ee153433587 (accessed June 2025); Danielle Douglas-Gabriel, "Graham Holdings swings to loss due to fallout from for-profit education," Washington Post, Nov. 5, 2015, https://www.washingtonpost.com/business/capitalbusiness/graham-holdings-swings-to-loss-due-to-fallout-from-for-profit-education/2015/11/05/cad3c390-83ed-11e5-8ba6-cec48b74b2a7_story.html (accessed June 2025); The Washington Post Company, "Form 10-K 2011," https://www.sec.gov/Archives/edgar/data/104889/000010488912000006/d10k.htm (accessed June 2025).

13. Permanent Equity, "Rule #1: Do No Harm," https://www.permanentequity.com/content/rule-1-do-no-harm (accessed June 2025); Permanent Equity, "How to Acquire Your First Small(er) Company," https://www.permanentequity.com/content/how-to-acquire-your-first-smaller-company (accessed June 2025).
14. Constellation Software Inc., "Q3 2023 Shareholders' Report (MD&A)," seller financing tools, https://www.csisoftware.com/docs/default-source/investor-relations/statutory-filings/csi---mda-q3-2023---final.pdf (accessed June 2025).
15. HEICO Corporation, "2023 Annual Report on Form 10-K," https://heico.com/wp-content/uploads/2024/04/AnnualReport_2023.pdf (accessed June 2025).
16. TransDigm Group Inc., "FY 2024 Form 10-K," https://www.transdigm.com/investor-relations/annual-reports/ (accessed June 2025); TransDigm Group Inc., "Fiscal 2024 Fourth Quarter and Year-End Results," press release, https://transdigmgroupinc.gcs-web.com/node/20716/pdf (accessed June 2025).
17. Danaher Corporation, "Danaher Business System Overview," investor presentation, May 2018, https://filecache.investorroom.com/mr5ir_danaher/507/Danaher%20DBS%20Overview%20May%202018.pdf (accessed June 2025).
18. Markel Group Inc., "2024 Shareholder Letter," https://content.markel.com/api/public/content/shareholder-letter-2024 (accessed June 2025); Markel Group Inc., "2024 Annual Report," https://s202.q4cdn.com/749045284/files/doc_financials/2024/ar/aa66a213-e8cd-46fd-9ab2-d69d655000b4.pdf (accessed June 2025).
19. Berkshire Hathaway Inc., "2025 Proxy Statement (DEF 14A)," compensation discussion noting Warren Buffett's salary and absence of stock-based compensation, https://www.berkshirehathaway.com/meet01/2025proxystatement.pdf (accessed June 2025).

20. Constellation Software Inc., "2025 Management Information Circular (Notice of Meeting)," executive bonus metrics, https://www.csisoftware.com/docs/default-source/press-releases/csi-mic-en.pdf (accessed June 2025); Constellation Software Inc., "Exhibit 26," SEC filing describing historical cash-bonus plans and required share purchases, https://www.sec.gov/Archives/edgar/data/1113678/000119312515138334/d906182dex26.htm (accessed June 2025).

21. United States Code, 26 U.S.C. § 1501, "Consolidated returns," Government Publishing Office, https://www.govinfo.gov/content/pkg/USCODE-2012-title26/pdf/USCODE-2012-title26-subtitleA-chap6-subchapA-sec1501.pdf (accessed June 2025).

22. United States Code, 26 U.S.C. § 243, "Dividends received by corporations," Government Publishing Office, https://www.govinfo.gov/content/pkg/USCODE-2012-title26/pdf/USCODE-2012-title26-subtitleA-chap1-subchapB-partVIII-sec243.pdf (accessed June 2025); Code of Federal Regulations, 26 C.F.R. § 1.243-1, Electronic Code of Federal Regulations, https://www.ecfr.gov/current/title-26/section-1.243-1 (accessed June 2025).

23. United States Code, 26 U.S.C. § 163(j), "Limitation on business interest," Government Publishing Office, https://www.govinfo.gov/content/pkg/USCODE-2012-title26/pdf/USCODE-2012-title26-subtitleA-chap1-subchapB-partVI-sec163.pdf (accessed v 2025); Code of Federal Regulations, 26 C.F.R. § 1.163(j)-2, Electronic Code of Federal Regulations, https://www.ecfr.gov/current/title-26/section-1.163(j)-2 (accessed June 2025).

24. California Franchise Tax Board, Publication 1061: Guidelines for Corporations Filing a Combined Report, https://www.ftb.ca.gov/forms/2022/2022-1061-publication.pdf (accessed June 2025).

25. California Franchise Tax Board, Regulation § 25136-2: Market-based sourcing for services and intangibles, draft text and ISOR, https://www.ftb.ca.gov/tax-pros/law/regulatory-activity/25136-2%20draft%20text.pdf; https://www.ftb.ca.gov/tax-pros/law/regulatory-activity/25136-2-ISOR.pdf (accessed June 2025).

26. Internal Revenue Service, About Form 8883 — Asset Allocation Statement Under Section 338, https://www.irs.gov/forms-pubs/about-form-8883 (accessed June2025); Internal Revenue Service, Instructions for Form 8883, https://www.irs.gov/pub/irs-pdf/i8883.pdf (accessed June 2025).

27. Internal Revenue Service, Like-Kind Exchanges — Real estate tax tips (IRC § 1031 overview), https://www.irs.gov/businesses/small-businesses-self-employed/like-kind-exchanges-real-estate-tax-tips (accessed June 2025).

28. United States Code, 26 U.S.C. § 1202, "Partial exclusion for gain from certain small business stock," Government Publishing Office, https://www.govinfo.gov/content/pkg/USCODE-2012-title26/pdf/USCODE-2012-title26-subtitleA-chap1-subchapP-partII-sec1202.pdf (accessed June 2025).

Chapter VIII: Compensation and Incentive Structures in Opco and Holdco Leadership

1. Constellation Software Inc., Annual Information Form 2024 (Toronto: Constellation, 2025), "Executive Compensation," https://www.csisoftware.com/category/stat-filings (accessed June 2025).

2. Danaher Corporation, Proxy Statement 2025 (Washington, DC: Danaher, 2025), "Executive Compensation Highlights," https://filecache.investorroom.com/mr5ir_danaher/919/download/Danaher%202025%20Proxy%20Statement.pdf (accessed June 2025).

3. Berkshire Hathaway Inc., Annual Report 2024 (Omaha, NE: Berkshire Hathaway, 2025), "Chairman's Letter," https://www.berkshirehathaway.com/letters/2024ltr.pdf (accessed June 2025).
4. Matt Foran, interview by David Weisburd, *How I Invest with David Weisburd*, episode 187, "Why Holding Companies Beat Private Equity," July 16, 2025, How I Invest Podcast, https://howiinvestpodcast.com/episodes/bBJkmhQMjlB (accessed July 2025).

Chapter IX: When Holdcos Fail: Patterns, Signals, and Lessons

1. Tyco International Ltd., Form 8-K, "Report of Investigations of Issues Raised by SEC Staff," December 30, 2002, U.S. SEC EDGAR, https://www.sec.gov/Archives/edgar/data/833444/000095013002008787/d8k.htm (accessed June 2025).
2. Tyco International Ltd., Amendment No. 2 to Form 10-K for the fiscal year ended September 30, 2002 (filed July 29, 2003), "Liquidity and Capital Resources," U.S. SEC EDGAR, https://www.sec.gov/Archives/edgar/data/833444/000104746903025320/a2113549z10-ka.htm (accessed June 2025). Figures referenced include total debt of $24.2058 billion and net debt of ~$18.0201 billion as of September 30, 2002.
3. U.S. Securities and Exchange Commission, "Complaint: SEC v. Tyco International Ltd., L. Dennis Kozlowski, Mark H. Swartz, and Mark A. Belnick," April 17, 2006, https://www.sec.gov/files/litigation/complaints/2006/comp19657.pdf (accessed June 2025).
4. Auburn University, Center for Ethical Organizational Cultures, "Tyco International: Leadership Crisis," case study, https://harbert.auburn.edu/binaries/documents/center-for-ethical-organizational-cultures/cases/tyco.pdf (accessed June 2025).

5. Valeant Pharmaceuticals International, Inc., DEF 14A (Management Proxy Circular and Proxy Statement), April 28, 2016, "Our 2015 annual incentive cash bonus program… based on… Adjusted EPS non-GAAP and revenue," U.S. SEC EDGAR, https://www.sec.gov/Archives/edgar/data/885590/000119312516567037/d166833ddef14a.htm (accessed June 2025).

6. New Constructs, "Today's 40% Drop Is Not Enough for Valeant Pharmaceuticals (VRX)," March 15, 2016, https://www.newconstructs.com/todays-40-drop-enough-valeant-pharmaceuticals/ (accessed June 2025).

7. Reuters, "Valeant CEO cuts outlook for 'distracted' company, shares plunge," June 7, 2016, https://www.reuters.com/article/business/valeant-ceo-cuts-outlook-for-distracted-company-shares-plunge-idUSKCN0YT122/ (accessed June 2025); Institutional Investor, "The Morning Brief: Valeant Is Now Trading Below $10," April 6, 2017, https://www.institutionalinvestor.com/article/2bsvrsnso5yacc2r0euww/portfolio/the-morning-brief-valeant-is-now-trading-below-10 (accessed June 2025).

8. Business Insider, "In leaked memo, Thrasio announces significant layoffs and a new CEO as the Amazon aggregator space slows," May 2, 2022, https://www.businessinsider.com/thrasio-layoffs-new-ceo-amazon-aggregator-2022-5 (accessed June 2025).

9. Reuters, "Amazon aggregator Thrasio files for bankruptcy," February 28, 2024, https://www.reuters.com/markets/deals/amazon-aggregator-thrasio-files-bankruptcy-2024-02-28/ (accessed June 2025).

10. Reuters, "Amazon-aggregator Thrasio emerges from bankruptcy, appoints CEO," June 18, 2024, https://www.reuters.com/technology/amazon-aggregator-thrasio-emerges-bankruptcy-appoints-ceo-2024-06-18/ (accessed June 2025).

11. General Electric Company, Annual Report 2007, PDF, https://www.annualreports.com/HostedData/AnnualReportArchive/g/NYSE_GE_2007.pdf (accessed June 2025). See "GECS Data," which reports GE Capital earnings from continuing operations of $12.428 billion versus consolidated earnings from continuing operations of $22.468 billion.
12. General Electric Company, Annual Report 2007, "Financial Resources and Liquidity," noting $101.1 billion of commercial paper outstanding at year-end 2007 and GE Capital debt-to-equity of 8.10:1, PDF, https://www.annualreports.com/HostedData/AnnualReportArchive/g/NYSE_GE_2007.pdf (accessed June 2025).
13. ProPublica, "General Electric Tapped Fed To Borrow $16 Billion," December 2, 2010, https://www.propublica.org/article/general-electric-tapped-fed-to-borrow-16-billion (accessed June 2025).
14. ProPublica, "How a Loophole Benefits General Electric in Bank Rescue," June 28, 2009, https://www.propublica.org/article/how-a-loophole-benefits-general-electric-628 (accessed June 2025).

Chapter XI: Private Equity's Holdco Evolution

1. Global Atlantic Financial Group, "KKR Completes Acquisition of Remaining 37% of Global Atlantic," January 2, 2024, https://www.globalatlantic.com/news/KKR-completes-acquisition-of-global-atlantic (accessed June 2025).
2. KKR & Co. Inc., "Insurance: Expertise in Managing Insurance Assets," https://www.kkr.com/invest/insurance (accessed June 2025).
3. Apollo Global Management, "Apollo Completes Merger with Athene and Finalizes Key Governance Enhancements," press release, January 3, 2022, https://www.apollo.com/insights-news/pressreleases/2022/01/apollo-completes-merger-with-athene-and-finalizes-key-governance-enhancements-120051006 (accessed June 2025).

4. Athene Holding Ltd., "Athene Announces Revised Investment Management Arrangements with Apollo Global Management," press release, September 20, 2018, https://ir.athene.com/news-events/press-releases/detail/105/athene-announces-revised-investment-management-arrangements-with-apollo-global-management (accessed June 2025).

5. Warren E. Buffett, "Berkshire Hathaway Shareholder Letters," Berkshire Hathaway Inc., https://www.berkshirehathaway.com/letters/letters.html (accessed June 2025).

6. Ares Management Corporation, "Infrastructure Opportunities," https://www.aresmgmt.com/our-business/infrastructure-opportunities (accessed June 2025); Ares Wealth Management Solutions, "Ares Core Infrastructure Fund (ACI)," https://www.areswms.com/solutions/aci (accessed June 2025).

7. Blackstone Inc., "BREIT | Blackstone Real Estate Income Trust," https://www.breit.com/ (accessed June 2025); Blackstone Inc., "Credit and Insurance (BXCI)," https://www.blackstone.com/our-businesses/credit-and-insurance-bxci/ (accessed June 2025).

8. Brookfield Corporation, "Brookfield Corporation Successfully Completes Distribution of 25% Interest in its Asset Management Business," press release, December 9, 2022, https://bam.brookfield.com/press-releases/brookfield-corporation-successfully-completes-distribution-25-interest-its-asset (accessed June 2025); Brookfield, "Who We Are," https://www.brookfield.com/about-us/who-we-are (accessed June 2025).

Chapter XII: Superacquirers

1. Accenture plc, "Accenture's acquisitions advantage," https://www.accenture.com/us-en/case-studies/about/accenture-acquisitions (accessed June 2025); Accenture plc, "Accenture Completes Acquisition of Work & Co," press release, January 22, 2024, https://newsroom.accenture.com/news/2024/accenture-completes-acquisition-of-global-digital-product-company-work-and-co (accessed June 2025).

2. S4 Capital plc, "Media.Monks Launch," press release, August 3, 2021, https://www.s4capital.com/data/production/2021-08/Media.Monks%20Launch%20_%20Press%20Release_0.pdf (accessed June 2025); PR Newswire, "Media.Monks ... refreshes brand to become Monks," July 18, 2024, https://www.prnewswire.com/news-releases/mediamonks-the-operating-brand-of-s4-capital-announces-strengthened-offerings-reflecting-accelerating-industry-transition-to-ai-powered-creative-and-technology-and-refreshes-brand-to-become-monks-302200039.html (accessed June 2025).

3. CGI Inc., "Mergers," https://www.cgi.com/en/mergers (accessed June 2025); CGI Inc., "CGI Management Foundation," https://www.cgi.com/en/about-us/cgi-management-foundation (accessed June 2025).

4. Capgemini SE, "Capgemini brings together its engineering and R&D expertise with the launch of new brand: 'Capgemini Engineering,'" press release, April 8, 2021, https://www.capgemini.com/news/press-releases/capgemini-brings-together-its-engineering-and-rd-expertise-with-the-launch-of-new-brand-capgemini-engineering (accessed June 2025).

5. Wipro Limited, "Wipro Announces a New Global Business Line Model to Deepen Alignment with Client Priorities," press release, February 27, 2023, https://www.wipro.com/newsroom/press-releases/2023/wipro-announces-new-global-business-line-model-to-deepen-alignment-with-client-priorities (accessed June 2025).

Chapter XIII: Creator Holdcos and Personal Holdcos

1. Los Angeles Times, "Shaquille O'Neal's business empire spans franchises, gyms, and real estate," August 2, 2023, https://www.latimes.com/entertainment-arts/story/2023-08-02/shaquille-oneal-business-empire (accessed June 2025).
2. Diageo plc, "Diageo to acquire Casamigos Tequila," press release, June 21, 2017, https://www.diageo.com/en/news-and-media/diageo-to-acquire-casamigos-tequila (accessed June 2025).
3. Greg Norman Company, "About," https://www.gregnorman.com (accessed June 2025); Greg Norman Estates, "Our Wines," https://www.gregnormanestateswine.com (accessed June 2025).
4. Feastables, "About Feastables," https://www.feastables.com (accessed June 2025); Restaurant Business Online, "MrBeast says he's 'moving on' from MrBeast Burger," June 18, 2023, https://www.restaurantbusinessonline.com/financing/mrbeast-says-hes-moving-mrbeast-burger (accessed June 2025); TechCrunch, "MrBeast's analytics platform ViewStats launches in beta," December 14, 2023, https://techcrunch.com/2023/12/14/mrbeasts-analytics-platform-viewstats-launches-in-beta (accessed June 2025).
5. Business Insider, "MrBeast's business empire hit $473 million in 2024 revenue and could reach $899 million by 2025, leaked deck shows," April 13, 2025, https://www.businessinsider.com/mrbeast-business-revenue-leaked-deck-2025-4 (accessed June 2025).

6. Sidemen, "Sides," https://www.eatsides.com (accessed June 2025); Sidemen, "XIX Vodka," https://xixvodka.com (accessed June 2025); Sidemen, "Sidemen Clothing," https://www.sidemenclothing.com (accessed June 2025); Sidemen, "Side+," https://www.sideplus.com (accessed June 2025).
7. The Times, "Sidemen launch venture capital firm Upside VC," May 2025, https://www.thetimes.co.uk/article/sidemen-launch-venture-capital-firm-upside-vc-2025 (accessed June 2025); Companies House, "Upside VC Limited, Company No. 14925725," https://find-and-update.company-information.service.gov.uk/company/14925725 (accessed June 2025).
8. Chamberlain Coffee, "About," https://chamberlaincoffee.com (accessed June 2025); Eater LA, "Emma Chamberlain is opening her first coffee shop," January 31, 2025, https://la.eater.com/2025/1/31/emma-chamberlain-coffee-shop-opening (accessed June 2025).
9. Fast Company, "Inside Marques Brownlee's tech review studio," November 14, 2023, https://www.fastcompany.com/90965767/mkbhd-tech-review-studio (accessed June 2025); Marques Brownlee, "MKBHD," https://mkbhd.com (accessed June 2025).
10. Sahil Bloom, "The Curiosity Chronicle," https://www.sahilbloom.com/newsletter (accessed June 2025); Sahil Bloom, "About," https://www.sahilbloom.com/about (accessed June 2025).
11. xAI, "Introducing Grok," November 3, 2023, https://x.ai/blog/introducing-grok (accessed June 2025); Reuters, "Elon Musk's xAI raises funds, integrates Grok into X," December 2024, https://www.reuters.com/technology/elon-musks-xai-integrates-grok-x-2024-12-12 (accessed June 2025).

12. Michael Karnjanaprakorn, "The Personal Holding Company," https://mikekarnj.com/personal-holding-company (accessed June 2025).
13. Michael Girdley, "About," https://girdley.com/about (accessed June 2025); Mineola Search Partners, "Founder interview: Michael Girdley," January 3, 2024, https://www.mineolasearch.com/blog/michael-girdley (accessed June 2025).
14. Contrarian Thinking, "About," https://contrarianthinking.co/about (accessed June 2025); Business Insider, "Codie Sanchez is making millions buying boring businesses," April 17, 2023, https://www.businessinsider.com/codie-sanchez-boring-businesses-investing-laundromats-car-washes-2023-4 (accessed June 2025).
15. Nick Huber, "About," https://nickhuber.com (accessed June 2025); Bolt Storage, "About Us," https://boltstorage.com/about (accessed June 2025); First Class Founders, "About," https://www.firstclassfounders.com/about (accessed June 2025); They Got Acquired, "Crypto newsletter Milk Road sold," https://theygotacquired.com/content/milk-road-sold (accessed June 2025).

MORE HOLDCO RESOURCES

The following are additional reading and listening resources for those who'd like to dive deeper into the world of holdcos and specific companies.

Books

- *The Outsiders* – William Thorndike

    Eight case studies of CEOs who achieved outsized returns through unorthodox capital allocation and decentralized models.

- *Lessons from the Titans* – Scott Davis, Carter Copeland, Rob Wertheimer

    Case studies of large industrial companies (e.g., Danaher, Honeywell) that highlight how capital allocation, culture, and strategic discipline drive long-term performance. Essential reading for understanding operational holdcos.

- *Strategy Beyond the Hockey Stick* – Chris Bradley, Martin Hirt, Sven Smit

    A McKinsey-based framework for understanding corporate strategy through probabilities and power moves.

- *Capital Allocation: The Financials of a New England Textile Mill 1955–1985* – Jacob McDonough
  A detailed analysis of Buffett's early years at Berkshire Hathaway through the lens of financial statements.
- *Cable Cowboy* – Mark Robichaux
  An account of how John Malone transformed TCI from a regional operator into America's dominant cable empire through aggressive acquisitions and shrewd capital allocation.
- *The Compounders: From Small Acquisitions to Giant Shareholder Returns* – Oddbjørn Dybvad, Kjetil Nyland, Adnan Hadžiefendić
  An introduction to high-performing yet unheralded holding companies that have mastered capital allocation coupled with a decentralized operational approach.
- *Never Enough: From Barista to Billionaire* – Andrew Wilkinson
  A memoir by Tiny co-founder Andrew Wilkinson on how he came to build his holding company through trial and error.

Podcasts

- *50X.* "TransDigm Series." Four episodes released July–August 2022.
  This series explores TransDigm's business model, capital allocation, compensation philosophy, and long-term compounding through candid conversations with its leaders and investors.
- *Business Breakdowns.* Episode 97: "Constellation Software: Principled, Profitable, Permanent," February 16, 2023.
  A deep dive into Constellation Software's disciplined culture, acquisition engine, and compensation philosophy, through the lens of Chris Cerrone of Akre Capital.

- *Business Breakdowns.* Episode 150: "HEICO: Parts for Planes," February 21, 2024.

  A high-detail breakdown of HEICO's aerospace maintenance, repair, and overhaul (MRO) business, highlighting the Mendelson family's expansion of the firm into aircraft aftermarket niches by comparing its operating model with TransDigm.

- *Acquired.* Season 12, Episode 2: "LVMH: The Complete History & Strategy," February 21, 2023.

  A deep dive into how Bernard Arnault transformed a bankrupt textile company into LVMH, exploring the strategic brilliance, cultural nuance, and luxury-sector dominance that underpin the group's ascent.

- *Joys of Compounding.* Episode 18: "The Art of Compounding," featuring Mitch Rales (co-founder of Danaher), April 29, 2024.

  A deep discussion on decades-long compounding, continuous improvement, and the philosophy of long-term organizational success.

- *Invest Like the Best with Patrick O'Shaughnessy.* Episode: "Trish and James Higgins of Chenmark Capital: Permanent Equity," March 14, 2017.

  A conversation with Trish and James Higgins of Chenmark on building a permanent capital holding company.

- *Think Like an Owner.* Episode 76: "Brent Beshore – Building and Growing a Competitive Advantage at Permanent Equity," August 10, 2021.

  Brent Beshore (founder and CEO of Permanent Equity) discusses how the firm builds competitive advantage through marketing, operations, and long-term, margin-of-safety strategies.

Annual Letters

Annual letters are more than updates; they're long-form operating manuals. Read them not just to learn what happened, but how decisions were made and how capital was prioritized.

- Constellation Software Letters

  Investor letters by founder Mark Leonard, offering rare insights into disciplined capital allocation, decentralized structures, and long-term thinking.

  Available at: https://www.csisoftware.com/category/pres-letters

- Berkshire Hathaway Annual Letters

  Warren Buffett's legendary shareholder letters, spanning six decades, cover everything from compounding and capital allocation to governance philosophy.

  Available at: https://www.berkshirehathaway.com/letters/letters.html

- Enduring Ventures Annual Letters

  Annual reflections from Enduring Ventures, a modern holding company experimenting with permanent capital and multi-sector stewardship.

  Available at: https://www.enduring.ventures

- Permanent Equity Annual Letters

  Thoughtful letters by Brent Beshore and team, explaining their approach to buying and holding small businesses indefinitely.

  Available at: https://www.permanentequity.com/letters

APPENDIX

More Examples of Sector-Specific Holdcos

Marketing and Advertising Services Holdcos

The marketing and advertising sector has historically been highly fragmented, making it ripe for consolidation. Sector-specific holdcos in this space benefit from shared media buying power, centralized creative services, and data-driven synergies.

Company	Holdco Type	Notes
Stagwell Group	Operational Holdco	Public, digital-first platform. About seventy specialist agencies share a mar-tech and data spine, yet keep brand P&Ls, aiming for scale without network bureaucracy.
WPP	Operational Holdco	Legacy global giant. Over 300 creative, media, and PR shops under regional clusters, with shared finance and procurement but wide operating autonomy.
Next 15 Group	Capital Allocator Holdco	UK-listed, this group reinvests cash flow into PR, data, and consulting boutiques at single-digit EBITDA multiples, integrating lightly and tracking ROIC by vintage.

| Project Worldwide | Capital Allocator Holdco | Employee-owned, this experiential and creative network features permanent equity, decentralized culture, and no exit clock. Their growth is funded from retained earnings. |

Consumer Brands Holdcos

Consumer brands holdcos leverage trusted brands, economies of distribution, and marketing scale. They often operate decentralized brand portfolios while seeking supply chain and operational efficiencies.

Company	Holdco Type	Notes
LVMH Moët Hennessy Louis Vuitton	Capital Allocator Holdco	Includes over seventy-five semi-autonomous luxury "maisons" across fashion, wines and spirits, jewelry, retail, and hospitality. The Arnault family allocates cash from mature houses into new labels and marquee deals (e.g., Tiffany) while sharing real-estate, manufacturing, and e-commerce infrastructure.
Procter & Gamble	Operational Holdco	This household- and personal-care giant features central R&D, supply chain, and media buying support-category P&Ls that each run their own brand playbooks.
Church & Dwight	Capital Allocator Holdco	A mid-cap CPG compounder, Church & Dwight funnels free cash into small-brand bolt-ons (OxiClean, Waterpik) at single-digit EBITDA multiples, integrating through a lean shared-services platform.
Estée Lauder Companies	Operational Holdco	This global beauty house acquires prestige and indie cosmetics lines, then folds them into a central marketing, distribution, and innovation engine while preserving brand identities.

| Sazerac Company | Capital Allocator Holdco | A family-owned spirits group, it has permanent capital funds and the long-horizon stewardship of Buffalo Trace, Fireball, and regional bourbon labels with decentralized storytelling and shared bottling logistics. |

Home Services Holdcos

Home services such as HVAC, plumbing, and electrical are highly localized and recession-resilient. Sector holdcos focus on geographic expansion, brand roll-ups, and operational excellence to build regional powerhouses.

Company	Holdco Type	Notes
TurnPoint Services	Operational Holdco	National HVAC, plumbing, and electrical platform backed by PE; has bought over forty founder-run contractors since 2016, keeps local names, and adds centralized dispatch, purchasing, and marketing to build a regional network.
Rollins Inc.	Operational Holdco	Orkin and sister pest-control brands are tightly integrated under a single operating playbook; growth comes from bolt-ons that are folded into common systems rather than managed as stand-alone units.
FirstService Corp.	Capital Allocator Holdco	Founder-led and publicly traded, FirstService Corp reinvests permanent capital into a family of adjacent service brands while letting each brand keep its own P&L discipline. Combines light central services with an allocator mindset.
Chemed Corp.	Capital Allocator Holdco	Owns two unrelated, independently run verticals—Roto-Rooter (plumbing) and VITAS (hospice). Capital is allocated across distinct industries, fitting the classic multi-segment conglomerate model.

B2B Services Holdcos

B2B services such as finance, IT, and professional services offer recurring revenue and sticky client relationships. Sector holdcos here often integrate back-office operations to scale profitably while retaining boutique service models.

Company	Holdco Type	Notes
Markel Ventures	Capital Allocator Holdco	This is the permanent-capital arm of Markel Group. It acquires family-owned outsourcing, consulting, and industrial-service firms, leaves brands independent, and measures success by look-through FCF and ROIC by vintage rather than EBITDA synergies.
Consero Global	Operational Holdco	A finance-as-a-service platform that centralizes controller, FP&A, and ERP tooling for mid-market clients; bolt-ons are fully integrated into one delivery stack to gain utilization and data visibility.
Converge One	Operational Holdco	An IT and unified-communications integrator that has completed over twenty acquisitions under successive PE sponsors; products, sales ops, and vendor contracts are progressively consolidated to chase scale economics.
Evergreen Services Group	Capital Allocator Holdco	Alpine-backed, this is a buy-and-hold aggregator of managed-service providers (MSPs). Local CEOs retain equity and autonomy while Evergreen supplies shared recruiting, vendor pricing, and KPI benchmarking.
RELX	Capital Allocator Holdco	This global information-services giant (LexisNexis, Elsevier, Risk Solutions) allocates capital across four semi-independent segments, funding data-set and analytics bolt-ons from a highly cash-generative core.

Software and SaaS Holdcos

Software and SaaS holdcos acquire sticky, mission-critical software companies with high gross margins and low churn. These businesses benefit from long product lifecycles and compound cash flows efficiently over time.

Company	Holdco Type	Notes
Constellation Software	Capital Allocator Holdco	A public, buy-and-hold acquirer of vertical-market software. Over 800 business units run autonomously with minimal HQ. Cash is redeployed into new deals that must clear a 20 percent hurdle rate.
Trilogy/ESW Capital	Operational Holdco	A private group that centralizes acquired B2B software into one cost-focused delivery stack—shared engineering, support, and aggressive margin expansion under a single P&L.
ASG (Alpine Software Group)	Capital Allocator Holdco	Alpine Investors have an evergreen platform. They buy founder-led SaaS, retain CEOs with equity rollovers, and layer on shared GTM playbooks while benchmarking ROIIC by acquisition vintage.
SureSwift Capital	Capital Allocator Holdco	A bootstrapped micro-SaaS collector with permanent capital, a remote team, and lightweight oversight aimed at reliable cash flow from dozens of $200k–$2M ARR products.
Roper Technologies	Capital Allocator Holdco	NYSE-listed industrial-tech group that has tilted 60 percent or more of revenue to mission-critical SaaS (Aderant, Deltek, iPipeline), allocating capital across unrelated verticals under one balance sheet.

Healthcare Services Holdcos

Healthcare services holdcos focus on consolidating clinics, physician groups, and specialty care providers. They benefit from aging demographics, growing demand, and the ability to professionalize smaller healthcare operations.

Company	Holdco Type	Notes
UnitedHealth Group (Optum)	Operational Holdco	This combines payer, PBM, and multi-specialty provider assets under one operating playbook. M&A is folded into Optum's tech, claims, and population-health stack to capture end-to-end margins.
The Ensign Group	Capital Allocator Holdco	A public nursing-facility buyer that decentralizes operations into over 300 locally run "service centers." HQ measures success by facility-level ROIC and lets strong operators reinvest cash in new sites.
Privia Health	Capital Allocator Holdco	In this physician-enablement platform, doctors keep ownership in their practices while Privia supplies population-health contracts, analytics, and revenue-cycle tools. There is a light central staff, and permanent capital.
EyeSouth Partners	Operational Holdco	This ophthalmology and retina practice aggregator is backed by private equity. Rapid add-ons are integrated into a shared back office, but brands remain local—aimed at a three- to five-year recap window.
CVS Health	Operational Holdco	This pharmacy giant turned healthcare conglomerate allocates capital across retail pharmacies, Aetna insurance, Caremark PBM, home health (Signify), and primary care (Oak Street), while reporting segment P&Ls.

Infrastructure and Utilities Holdcos

Infrastructure and utilities are attractive for their long-term contracts, inflation-linked revenues, and defensible assets. Holdcos here own and operate critical infrastructure like energy pipelines, ports, and data centers.

Company	Holdco Type	Notes
Brookfield Infrastructure Partners	Capital Allocator Holdco	A global owner of toll roads, ports, data centers, and mid-stream pipes that raises permanent/evergreen capital and redeploys free cash into new assets that must clear a 12 to 15 percent equity IRR hurdle.
Berkshire Hathaway Energy	Capital Allocator Holdco	This holdco houses eight regulated electric and gas utilities, a long-haul transmission business, and wind/solar pipelines. Capital flows among segments, but each utility keeps its own regulated rate base and board.
NextEra Energy Partners	Capital Allocator Holdco	This NYSE-listed "yieldco" is spun from NextEra. It drops down wind, solar, and natural-gas pipelines into separate opcos while keeping a lean parent that targets 12 to 15 percent dividend-per-share growth via acquisitions.
Algonquin Power and Utilities	Operational Holdco	A public utility consolidator, it funds serial acquisitions of municipal water, gas, and electric systems plus wind/solar assets, aiming for double-digit rate-base growth—high leverage and rate-case execution are key risks.
Clearway Energy Inc.	Operational Holdco	This holdco owns eight GW of contracted wind, solar, and gas plants. Centralized asset-management and merchant hedging desks run the fleet, while growth comes from tuck-in project acquisitions funded with dropdown cash.

Real Estate Holdcos

Real estate holdcos aggregate residential, commercial, or industrial properties to generate recurring rental income and asset appreciation. Operational excellence in property management is critical to driving returns.

Company	Holdco Type	Notes
Brookfield Property Partners	Capital Allocator Holdco	A flagship property arm of Brookfield Corp., it recycles proceeds from mature assets into new office, retail, logistics, and data-center projects, targeting 12 to 15 percent equity IRR while leaving day-to-day ops to local teams.
Invitation Homes	Operational Holdco	This NYSE-listed owner and operator of over 80k single-family rental homes across the Sunbelt functions as an operational holdco with centralized systems for maintenance, leasing, and procurement. Their growth strategy focuses on infill acquisitions that enhance portfolio density, enabling operating leverage and long-term yield optimization.
Tricon Residential	Operational Holdco	Tricon is a Toronto-listed owner-operator of SFR and multifamily units. It partners with pension funds in JVs, keeps neighborhood-level property managers, and recycles its promote (carried interest) into new development.
Greystar	Operational Holdco	A founder-owned global multifamily giant, Greystar boasts permanent GP capital. Co-investment LPs fuel a vertically integrated platform spanning development, construction, and management of over 800k units.
Blackstone Real Estate Income Trust (BREIT)	Capital Allocator Holdco	Non-traded, this perpetual-life vehicle raises retail capital to acquire stabilized apartments, logistics, and self-storage. This holdco has 60 to 65 percent asset-level leverage that supports a roll-up model with optional exits.

Education Holdcos

Education-focused holdcos invest in for-profit schools, online learning platforms, and vocational training companies. These holdcos often modernize legacy education assets and benefit from increasing demand for reskilling.

Company	Holdco Type	Notes
Stride Inc. (formerly K12)	Operational Holdco	A public online-learning platform with central curriculum, tech, and marketing that powers a network of virtual K–12 schools plus adult-career programs, with tuck-ins fully integrated under one P&L.
Cambium Learning Group	Operational Holdco	This Veritas-backed ed-tech platform owns Lexia, Voyager Sopris, Time4Learning, and Rosetta Stone. It acquires niche curriculum and assessment tools, then shares sales ops and product R&D to lift margins before the next recap.
Strada Education Network	Capital Allocator Holdco	This holdco converts endowment returns into equity stakes in skills-training, career-navigation, and student-success tech. Their portfolio companies operate autonomously while Strada supplies research grants and long-horizon capital—no exit clock.
Laureate Education	Capital Allocator Holdco	A NASDAQ-listed owner of private universities in Mexico and Peru; their local leadership keeps academic autonomy while HQ allocates capital, negotiates financing, and shares student-recruitment tech across campuses.

Industrial Holdcos

Industrial holdcos acquire specialized manufacturers that produce mission-critical components. They thrive on decentralized operations, deep technical expertise, and durable customer relationships across economic cycles.

Company	Holdco Type	Notes
Danaher Corporation	Operational Holdco	Danaher runs over twenty life-science and industrial platforms under the Danaher Business System. Bolt-ons are folded into common lean-production playbooks to drive margin lift and cash conversion.
TransDigm Group	Capital Allocator Holdco	A highly leveraged buyer of proprietary aerospace components, their 100-plus units stay autonomous. Free cash plus recap debt is recycled into new deals that must clear a mid-teens IRR hurdle.
HEICO Corporation	Capital Allocator Holdco	A family-controlled aerospace and electronics group, HEICO acquires niche suppliers, leaves founders in place, and shares purchasing power while tracking ROIIC by vintage.
Addtech AB	Operational Holdco	This Stockholm-listed distributor of high-spec industrial components has more than 140 micro-subsidiaries. It keeps local brands but pools back-office systems. It targets between ten and fifteen add-ons a year.
Illinois Tool Works (ITW)	Capital Allocator Holdco	ITW has over eighty decentralized specialty-manufacturing businesses running on the 80/20 focus rule. Capital is allocated across unrelated end-markets with a century-long dividend record.

Restaurant Group Holdcos

Restaurant holdcos collect franchised or company-owned dining concepts under one roof. They monetize brand equity, scale purchasing, and shared tech platforms, while diversification across dayparts, price points, and formats smooths cash flow through cycles.

Company	Holdco Type	Notes
Restaurant Brands International	Capital Allocator Holdco	Royalty-rich, this asset-light owner of Burger King, Tim Hortons, Popeyes, and Firehouse Subs redeploys franchise cash into buy-backs, bolt-ons, and store remodel capex cleared by a 12 percent or more IRR hurdle.
Darden Restaurants	Operational Holdco	Darden runs over 1,900 company-owned casual chains (Olive Garden, LongHorn, Cheddar's). Its margins are lifted via centralized purchasing, labor analytics, and real-estate science while each banner controls menu and marketing.
Inspire Brands (Roark Capital)	Operational Holdco	This holdco mixes 32k franchised and company units (Arby's, Dunkin', Sonic, Buffalo Wild Wings). The light HQ supplies drive-thru tech, loyalty apps, and bulk ingredients while local operators keep P&L accountability. It is PE-backed, but with a long hold philosophy.
FAT Brands	Operational Holdco	A debt-heavy franchisor that has scooped up over fifteen concepts (Johnny Rockets, Twin Peaks, Fazoli's) since 2017. Brands remain distinct but share development, supply chain, and finance teams ahead of a future recap.
Jollibee Group	Capital Allocator Holdco	This family-controlled Filipino QSR group features permanent capital funds. The global expansion of Jollibee plus The Coffee Bean & Tea Leaf and Smashburger lets regional CEOs drive menu localization and unit growth.

ACKNOWLEDGEMENTS

The idea for this book first came when Greg Alexander, founder of the professional services community Collective 54 and author of *The Boutique*, emailed me asking for a recommendation of materials around holding companies.

In compiling a brief email for Greg with some books, podcasts, and blog posts, I realized that it was hard to pinpoint a cohesive piece of writing that spanned many different source materials.

This was also at a time when I was continually refining the strategy and structure for Barrel Holdings, my holding company that acquires and grows specialized digital and marketing agencies.

I decided to take a crack at writing a more comprehensive guide for my fellow entrepreneurs. My initial goal was a five to ten-page e-book that I could share as a PDF. Before I knew it, I had written dozens of pages with more sections I wanted to cover. So thank you, Greg, for the initial inspiration.

Thanks to my Barrel Holdings co-founder Sei-Wook, my close friend and business partner of over twenty-plus years, for being a perpetual thought partner and source of encouragement and support. Thank you to all of those who read drafts of this book at various stages and provided valuable feedback including Walter Chen, Matt Graham, and Josh Nissenboim.

I'm also grateful to the dozens of agency founders who've reached out to inquire about the Barrel Holdings model over the past couple of years. Each rep has allowed me to sharpen the story and become more confident in the model we are pursuing.

And finally, much thanks and love to my family–my wife Melanie, my sons Grant, Teddy, and Xander, my parents, and my sister Dawn–all of you made this book possible.

ABOUT THE AUTHOR

PETER KANG is co-founder of Barrel Holdings, which acquires and grows specialized agency businesses. The portfolio includes Barrel, a leading Shopify agency, and BX Studio, a leading Webflow agency.

Peter enjoys working closely with agency leaders both in and outside of Barrel Holdings, being a sounding board, and sharing lessons learned from years of being an agency operator. He also runs AgencyHabits, a business and leadership resource for agency leaders.

Peter resides in the Hudson Valley, north of New York City, with his wife and three boys.

For more information, visit:

- www.peterkang.com
- www.barrel-holdings.com
- www.agencyhabits.com

Made in the USA
Middletown, DE
24 February 2026

28566390R00085